中國烹飪藝術

The Art of Chinese Cooking

By

Rebekah Lin Jewell

For comments and questions, please visit
www.artofchinesecooking.com

AuthorHouse™
1663 Liberty Drive, Suite 200
Bloomington, IN 47403
www.authorhouse.com
Phone: 1-800-839-8640

First published by AuthorHouse 1/9/2009

ISBN: 978-1-4389-0217-3 (sc)

Printed in the United States of America
Bloomington, Indiana

This book is printed on acid-free paper.

For my family

Contents

INTRODUCTION

In China, there is an old proverb: Food is the first necessity of man 民以食為天. That is to say, food plays a very important role in our everyday lives. Over time, people around the world have celebrated the importance of food, and countries have developed their own unique cuisines and specialties. Today, Chinese cuisine is one of the most popular foods in the world.

My father, who worked for the Chinese postal service in the early 1920s in Beijing, was very fond of good food. My mother, a devoted wife, cooked nearly every meal for my father. Moving to Urumqi 烏魯木齊, Xinjiang 新疆 Province, and then to Nanning 南寧, Guangxi 廣西 Province, my family was well traveled in China before I was born. My brother and sisters often told me how affluent we were before the communists took over. Since my mother was a terrific cook who entertained friends and guests frequently, I learned to appreciate good food at a very young age.

Nevertheless, growing up in Taiwan, I was never really interested in cooking. Being the youngest in the family, I was quite spoiled and seldom needed in the kitchen. In 1962, after finishing college in Taipei, I went to Okinawa to visit my brother, who was working for the U.S. government. There I met my husband, Richard Jewell, a widower with three small children. After we married, I faced a sink-or-swim situation in the kitchen. The maid taught me how to cook a few simple dishes, such as beef stew, meat loaf, and spaghetti. But friends and relatives assumed that, since I was Chinese, I would naturally be able to prepare dishes from my native cuisine. I felt a sense of panic.

So I made up my mind that I was going to learn to be a good cook. Shortly after immigrating to the United States in 1964, I realized that, even though I wasn't yet an expert, I could do a decent job in the kitchen. I discovered that, if I tried very hard, I could conquer my fears. I immersed myself in several cookbooks, including the *Joy of Cooking*, which I considered to be my bible. My mother began sending me a variety of Chinese cookbooks for me to study. Since I knew what a well-prepared dish should taste like, I'd start by following the recipe, then experiment until I got the taste right. In 1969, my family and I moved to England, where I had more opportunities to cook for friends. I felt satisfied and encouraged when my guests praised the meals I prepared. I began to realize that I had a genuine talent and love for cooking.

In 1972, we moved back to Okinawa and lived there for two more years. I heard that a Mrs. Huang, who had taken cooking lessons from a very well-known Chinese cooking instructor in Taiwan, was giving private Chinese cooking lessons. I organized a group of like-minded women, and we started studying with Mrs. Huang. My own kitchen became a classroom for almost two years. Those lessons under Mrs. Huang's tutelage gave me the confidence that I was following the right techniques in the kitchen.

When we moved to Fairfax, Virginia, in 1974, I continued to hone my Chinese cooking skills. I frequently entertained friends and started offering private cooking lessons out of my home. Then, in the late 1970s, I began teaching for Fairfax County Adult and Community Education. I also taught Chinese cooking for the Northern Virginia Community College extension program for two years. At present I teach for L'Academie de Cuisine, Sur La Table, Arlington Adult Education, and Fairfax County Adult and Community Education. Off and on, I have taught Chinese cooking for more than twenty-five years.

With encouragement from my family, friends, and students, I decided to compile a cookbook containing recipes that I have collected and fine-tuned over the years. The dishes that you'll discover in this book have brought much joy to my family, my students, and myself, and I hope they will do the same for you.

I want to thank my late mother, who gave me the opportunity to discover good food at a very young age; my husband Richard, who helped me transcribe my recipes over the years; and my son Christopher, who taught me how to use a computer. My thanks also to my daughters-in law Anna and Janice for proofreading the manuscript. Most of all, I want to thank my son Andrew. This book never would have been completed without his countless hours of meticulous editing, guidance, and encouragement.

MEMORIES OF MY YOUTH

Since this is my first – and probably only – book, I'd like to share some of my childhood memories. I realize that my childhood memories have little to do with a cookbook, but I want to pass them on to my children and grandchildren.

A plan to swap the babies

After fourteen years of marriage, my father and mother had one son and three daughters. In 1937, my mother was pregnant with me, her seventh child (a brother and sister had died before I was born). She was anxious to have another boy to carry the family name. Our next-door neighbor, Mrs. Dong, already had four sons, and she too was pregnant. Mrs. Dong, of course, was hoping for a little girl. So she and my mother secretly agreed that if a girl was born to the Lin family and a boy to the Dong family, they would swap the babies. Fortunately, my mother could not keep a secret, and she told my father about her great scheme. My father was livid and accused her of losing her mind. I often think about how different my life would have been if I had been exchanged for Mrs. Dong's child – who, by the way, turned out to be her fifth son. After we moved to Taiwan in 1949, we lost touch with the Dongs.

Sharing my biscuits

It was 1941. My best friend was Joy, whose parents were missionaries from Australia. We went to preschool twice a week. Miss Stevenson, a missionary from Ireland, accompanied us to and from school by foot. I must say those missionaries spoke flawless Mandarin and could write perfectly in Chinese. In those days we were required to wear a school-issued apron with a pocket on one side. We were given two biscuits for our mid-morning snack, and I always ate just one and kept the other in my pocket to give to our neighbor's toddler after school. I remember this vividly, even today. Perhaps that is why I still love to share my food and recipes with family, students, and friends.

Wet nurse

In China, it is impolite to address an older person by his or her first name, even if that person is your twin sibling born just ten minutes earlier than you! Thus, in our family, I call my oldest sister No. 1 sister, the second oldest No. 2 sister, and the third oldest No. 3 sister. My No. 1 sister, Helen, once told me that my parents were quite affluent and could afford to hire a wet nurse to nurse me for one year when we lived in Guangxi 廣西 Province. Perhaps that is why I've always felt so different from my siblings. After I watched the Oscar-winning movie *The Last Emperor*, I realized that one can become very attached to, and greatly influenced by, a wet nurse.

Fear of pockmarks

My parents moved to Guizhou 貴州 Province when I was three years old. I don't remember exactly at what age I learned to handle chopsticks skillfully, but I do recall eating plain boiled rice at least twice a day in a rice bowl. One day, when I was perhaps six or seven years old, we were all sitting around the table eating dinner. I probably didn't like the food and finished my meal very quickly, leaving a few grains of rice in the bowl. My mother told me very seriously that I would grow pockmarks on my face if I left any rice in the bowl. Strangely, over sixty years later I still eat every last grain of rice on my plate.

Marriage by matchmaker

The year was 1922, my father was a confirmed bachelor in his late twenties, living in Beijing, and my mother had just graduated from a well-known, exclusive girls school in Fujian 福建 Province. She was valedictorian of her class and had won a full scholarship to a prestigious university in Beijing. But my maternal grandfather, a medical doctor, died suddenly at the age of forty-five, leaving eight children for my grandmother to raise. My mother, who was the oldest child, had to give up her academic future to work and help support the family. My paternal uncle realized that an intelligent woman, dedicated to family, was needed to tame a wild-horse-type of man like my father. He arranged my parents' marriage through a matchmaker and paid my grandmother a large lump sum to help her raise the other children. For the rest of her life, my mother had a chip on her shoulder for all that she had to sacrifice for her family.

Unique tombstones

When I was in kindergarten, I loved to ask questions. One day I was looking at the family photo album, and I saw two pictures of very untraditional tombstones, designed like houses with roofs and doors. Names were engraved on the doors. I asked my mother who was inside the tombs. She said it was my brother and my sister who had died in Urumqi 烏魯木齊, Xinjiang 新疆 Province, before I was born. My next question, of course, was why they had to die. She told me that they had died of scarlet fever, and that because they were good children, God wanted them to go to heaven early. My mother's explanation had a tremendous impact on me as a young child. In fact, from that day on, I didn't want to be a perfect little girl because I was so afraid of dying.

Young thieves

When I was in third or fourth grade, living in Guiyang 貴陽, Guizhou 貴州 Province, I had a rich friend who lived across from me. We became good friends at school. In those days there was very little entertainment in my life, and I was often bored. Reading books was about the only fun thing I could do. My rich friend, on the other hand, could go to the movies and go dancing, and her family had a radio. My mother, who was a devout Southern Baptist, always said that going to the movies and dancing were sins. Near our home, there was a big farm where a farmer grew different crops depending on the season. One summer evening, my rich friend suggested that we steal some corn from the farmer after dark, just for a little fun. I was very scared, but my friend assured me that the farmer would never notice us, since the cornfield was very dense. The moment we entered the cornfield, however, the farmer turned on his flashlight and yelled, "Who's there?" My friend and I ran as fast as we could. This escapade occurred more than sixty years ago, yet I still remember it vividly. That was the only time in my life I tried to be a thief!

Gender in China

My husband can't understand why so many Chinese people, despite having lived in America almost all their lives, frequently mix up the personal pronouns "he" and "she." In simple conversations, we often say "he" instead of "she" when referring to a woman. The reason is because "she" doesn't exist in colloquial Chinese. However, Chinese people are very careful to distinguish gender among relatives and families. For example, in America, when grandparents are mentioned, you don't know whether they are from the father's side or the mother's side, but in China we have different words for paternal and maternal grandparents. Furthermore, for uncles and aunts, nephews and nieces, we have different words to specify which side of the family they're on. Among family members we have different words for older brother, younger brother, older sister, and younger sister. Perhaps that is why we don't use "she" in conversation.

Carrying the family name

In China, it is very important to have a son born into the family. There is an old saying: A son is needed to support you in your old age, but mainly he will carry your name from one generation to the next. There was a couple in our church in Guiyang 貴陽, Guizhou 貴州 Province, named Mr. and Mrs. Wong. They had only one child – a daughter – and desperately wanted to keep the surname Wong going. Before their daughter's marriage, the future son-in-law agreed that their odd-numbered children would carry his surname and their even-numbered children her surname. When we were in Sunday school, I was always puzzled why children from the same family had different surnames. By the way, Mr. and Mrs. Wong had six grandchildren: three boys and three girls.

My birthday treat

Before I came to the United States, I often heard that America was heaven for the young, a battlefield for the middle-aged, and a graveyard for the old. I've lived in America for almost forty years now, and I must say there is a little truth to this adage. In China we celebrate your birthday only after you turn fifty years old, and the older you get, the bigger the party is. When we were children, our mother would get up extra early on our birthdays and prepare us each a bowl of noodle soup and two hard-boiled eggs. Always very inquisitive, I would ask my mother, "Why the noodles and two hard-boiled eggs?" She said the noodles symbolized long life. As for the hard-boiled eggs, she had no clue what they represented, but said her mother always served them on her birthday when she was a child. One time I was talking about this birthday tradition in my cooking class, and a Chinese student said her grandmother had explained to her that a noodle represents the number one, and the two hard-boiled eggs represent two zeros. I finally understood that my traditional birthday meal was, in fact, a wish to live to age one hundred.

Chinese herbal medicine

The year was 1941 or 1942, I was five or six years old living in Guiyang 貴陽, Guizhou 貴州 Province, and the Japanese had invaded Manchuria. One spring evening my father informed us that the family must move to a village in the countryside called Qinxi 黔西, because the Japanese were approaching the southern provinces. My family packed in a hurry, and we traveled in a dilapidated, old-fashioned bus which used wood logs as fuel. That was the first time I had ridden a bus, and I was very sick. The bus constantly broke down, and it seemed to take days to reach our destination. I can't remember how long we stayed in the country, but I do remember that I was sick with chicken pox. There weren't any Western doctors in that tiny, remote village, so I had to take Chinese herbal medicine, which tasted bitter and awful. That was the last time I ever resorted to Chinese herbal remedies.

Our church organist

My father retired early from his postal service job and left mainland China for Taiwan in 1948 with my oldest brother David. My mother and her four daughters remained in Guiyang 貴陽, where we were invited to stay in a church. The church was quite large. I remember that we had three rooms and lived there comfortably. Meanwhile, my father was busy buying a house for the family in Tainan 台南, Taiwan. The Guiyang church had a large congregation, and Miss Ho was our organist. I don't remember what illness she had, but I remember she died very suddenly in her mid-twenties. Miss Ho was admired and loved, and her death was a great shock to all. It was the first time in my life that someone I felt very close to went to heaven so young. There was a big funeral and a memorial service at our church. I was forced to pay my respects to Miss Ho before an open coffin. I never imagined that a brief viewing of Miss Ho would haunt me for the rest of my life. I couldn't sleep that night, couldn't get her face out of my mind. In fact, I had many sleepless nights for several years. From that day on, I have never looked at a dead person in a coffin, not even my own father and mother.

Rival aunts

My mother was one of eight children: two sons and six daughters. The first time I met my second and eighth aunts was in 1949 in Fuzhou 福州. I couldn't understand why they all lived together in the same household. Each aunt had several children, yet the two sisters didn't speak to each other at all. I was also quite puzzled by the fact that my eighth aunt didn't have a husband. My mother explained to me that my eighth aunt was a concubine of the husband of my second aunt. Although I had read and heard tales about concubines in China, I couldn't believe there was one in my own family! That man (I called him Uncle) was a very busy person who divided his time between his two women.

My unusual maternal grandmother

When I met my grandmother for the first time in 1949 in Fuzhou 福州, she was visiting my rival aunts. She was in her early sixties, with gray hair, no teeth, and bound feet, and was a very kind and benevolent woman. One day she took me to her son's home where she was living. I was absolutely shocked when I walked into the living room. On display was a red coffin with its cover open. Ever since attending our church organist's funeral, I have tried very hard to avoid looking inside any coffin. I asked my grandmother why the coffin was there, and she proudly said that it was a gift from her son for her final day. When the communists took over mainland China and we moved to Taiwan, we lost touch with my grandmother. Many years later we heard that my uncle had died young and that my grandmother had lived into her nineties. Often I have wondered whether my uncle used that red coffin instead of my grandmother.

Last ship to leave Fujian

One day in the summer of 1949, my mother informed us that we must leave Fuzhou 福州 immediately to catch the very last ship sailing for Taiwan. Our household goods were still on the way to Fuzhou from Guiyang 貴陽, so we had to leave everything behind, including our precious family photos. At that time my second sister, Joy, was finishing her senior year of college in Sichuan 四川 Province. She ended up staying in mainland China, and it wasn't until 1981 that we were finally united in the United States after thirty-two years apart. Fortunately, Joy had saved a few family photos.

Barefoot in school

When I was living in mainland China, we always walked to school. So when we moved to Tainan 台南, walking to school again was nothing unusual. I'll never forget the first day of school. I was the only one wearing a pair of shoes. I was also terribly embarrassed because I was the tallest girl in the entire school. Everyone stared at me and looked surprised. I learned very quickly that I wasn't supposed to wear my shoes in school. For the entire sixth grade I walked to school with my shoes on and took them off when I arrived.

Cleaning girl at school

From junior high school through high school I attended all-girls schools in Tainan 台南. There were no custodians to clean up for us; we students were the cleaning crew. We cleaned our classroom and the principal's and teachers' offices daily after class. Since we were the cleaning ladies, we tried our best not to be messy in the first place.

My fifth aunt

My mother's fifth younger sister was married to a wealthy businessman for ten years. When he died, he left her a large fortune. I will never forget how she loved to play mah jong. She was addicted to this ancient Chinese game of chance. Some Chinese people take mah jong very seriously. My aunt would play mah jong continuously for up to twenty-four hours. In the end, she became a pauper and died of a heart attack at age fifty.

REGIONAL COOKING OF CHINA

Chinese cooking is divided into four distinctive schools, characterized primarily by a combination of geographical spices and sauces. Let's look more closely at the four schools.

Northern cooking

This includes the provinces of Shandong 山東, Hebei 河北, and Henan 河南. Today, when speaking of northern cooking, we mainly emphasize the Beijing style. Often abundant in garlic and green onions, this region's food is light as opposed to oily, mild as opposed to spicy. The most famous banquet dishes are Bird's Nest Soup (I don't teach this dish) and Peking Duck. Popular dishes in the United States, such as Hot and Sour Soup and Moo Shi Pork, are considered country cooking in China. Since the weather in northern China is suitable for growing wheat, daily meals in this region include noodles, dumplings, and buns.

Eastern cooking

This includes the provinces of Jiangsu 江蘇, Zhejiang 浙江, and Fujian 福建. The regional specialty is "red cooking" (cooking with soy sauce). In addition to soy sauce, salt or sugar (or a combination thereof) is used to enhance the taste, such as in Soy Sauce Chicken and Lion's Head. Since the eastern provinces are near the coast, seafood and vegetables are in abundance. Eastern cooking is rich but not as oily as western cooking. Fujian Province is well known for its outstanding seafood, rice noodles, and spring rolls.

Western cooking

The western region of China includes the provinces of Sichuan 四川, Hunan 湖南, Guizhou 貴州, Hubei 湖北, and Yunnan 雲南. Although the Guizhou, Hubei, and Yunnan schools of cooking have had an influence, western cooking is best known for the cuisines of Sichuan and Hunan. The most distinguishing feature of western cooking is its hot and spicy taste. Hot peppers are grown abundantly in Hunan Province and peppercorns in Sichuan Province. Hot spices are often mixed with minced ginger, garlic, and onions to enhance the flavor of the food. Daily meals make heavy use of spices, but formal banquets in Sichuan exclude hot and spicy courses. Sichuan Duck is an example of a non-spicy dish commonly served at banquets.

Southern cooking

Southern cooking is found in the provinces of Guangdong 廣東 and Guangxi 廣西. Guangdong cooking is undoubtedly the best-known Chinese cooking school in the world, partly because the province's citizens immigrated to countries around the globe. Guangdong Province became rich through foreign trade, and its wealthy people developed a desire for good food. Guangzhou 廣州, the capital of Guangdong, is the center of southern cooking. According to a Chinese proverb, if you like to eat good food, go to Guangzhou.

Guangdong dishes don't use many spices, but they do incorporate lots of oyster sauce and hoisin sauce. Examples are Beef with Broccoli and Chinese Roast Pork. Preparation relies heavily on quick stir-frying; hence a variety of Guangdong dishes are served in restaurants that offer take-out.

UTENSILS AND CUTTING

Wok

I had never heard of the word wok until I came to the United States in 1964. I was born in Nanning 南寧, Guangxi 廣西 Province. Most people in Nanning speak Cantonese, but my parents spoke Mandarin and Fujianese at home. Guo 鍋 is the Mandarin word for a rounded cooking pan. Nowadays, around the world, the Cantonese word wok – equivalent to guo – is the term used in Chinese cooking.

In all the years that I have been teaching, the question most frequently asked by my students is: "Do you need a wok to cook Chinese food?" My answer is always: "Not necessarily," because a western deep Dutch oven is a good substitute.

There are many different kinds of woks on the market, from the expensive, nonstick type to cast iron woks and cheap carbon steel woks. I love to use a cast iron wok, but it is too heavy for me to carry around to the different schools where I teach. Therefore, I normally use a carbon steel wok, which is thin and conducts heat very rapidly. It is ideal for stir-frying.

The wok is a very versatile piece of cookware. It can serve as a frying pan, saucepan, deep fryer, and even a steamer when used with a rack. A wok cover is quite handy for braising, stewing, and steaming; I highly recommend that you buy a wok with a cover.

A 14-inch-diameter, flat-bottomed wok with a single, long, straight handle made of wood is easier to use than a wok with handles on both sides. Some woks come with a metal ring that attaches to the underside of the wok to help stabilize it. I never use the ring, preferring instead to use a flat-bottomed wok that directly touches the burner.

A new wok should be seasoned by heating it over low heat until hot. Next, remove the wok from the heat, brush the inside surface with vegetable oil, and let sit for one minute. Wipe the wok clean with a wad of paper towels. Repeat this process three times. Now the wok is ready to use.

Always remember to heat a carbon steel or cast iron wok before adding oil. When the wok is hot, the pores of the metal will open, allowing the surface to absorb the oil. This way, the food won't stick to the wok, which is especially important when cooking meat or poultry coated with cornstarch. With a nonstick wok, on the other hand, do not heat the wok first before adding oil. Leaving a nonstick wok on high heat without oil will damage the nonstick coating.

It is very important to use soap and hot water to clean the wok after cooking. After the wok has been washed and rinsed, I highly recommend heating it in order to dry it thoroughly and prevent rusting. If you don't use the wok very often, it's also a good idea to oil the inside surface to prevent rusting.

Steamer

The steamer is considered an important utensil, second only to the wok and comparable to the oven in Western cooking. A steamer consists of a large pot, two tiers of steaming racks, and a cover. Some food can be steamed directly on the rack, while some needs to be put into a heatproof dish before placing it in the steamer.

9

There are two kinds of steamers that you can buy: bamboo and aluminum. Bamboo steamers are the best kind because less moisture forms on the lid during the steaming process. A bamboo steamer rests on a wok and should be 2 inches smaller in diameter than the wok. For example, for a 14-inch wok, you should buy a 12-inch steamer and use an 11-inch or smaller heatproof dish. If you are making any type of dim sum, line the rack with wet cheesecloth or parboiled cabbage. Since bamboo steamers are very difficult to clean when chicken or duck is placed directly on the rack, I often use an aluminum steamer for easy cleaning. Always bring the water to a vigorous boil before starting to steam.

If you don't have a steamer, you can save the empty, small cans of hot bean sauce or sweet bean sauce and open both ends. Put three or four cans in a wok or large pot, in an inch or more of water, and place a heatproof plate over them. There should be at least a 2-inch space between the water and the food to be steamed; otherwise, the boiling water might touch the food and ruin it. Cover with a tight-fitting lid and steam. Certain kinds of food require steaming for a long time. Boiling water in a wok or pot evaporates very quickly, so you need to replenish it frequently. Always have boiling water handy; never pour in cold water while steaming. To avoid scalding your fingers, be sure to use oven mitts to remove food from your steamer.

Chinese cleaver

The Chinese cleaver is essential in the preparation of Chinese food. Some of my students confuse it with the ordinary meat cleaver, which is used to cut through bones. The Chinese cleaver is used strictly for cutting food into uniform, bite-sized pieces, not for cutting thick bones. That kind of use will dull and eventually destroy the fine edge.

I've been using a Chinese cleaver ever since I married more than forty years ago. To me, the Chinese cleaver is one of the most versatile and indispensable tools in any kitchen. It is used for slicing, shredding, mincing, crushing, chopping, tenderizing, and roll cutting. I especially like the fact that you can use the flat side of the cleaver as a spatula to lift the cut pieces into a dish or a bowl.

There are two kinds of Chinese cleavers that you can buy in stores or through the Internet. It is true that a carbon steel cleaver is used by chefs worldwide and is easy to sharpen. I still prefer to use a cleaver made of stainless steel, mainly because it won't rust and is easier to take care of.

Never buy a cheap cleaver; it will be a total waste of money. Buy a quality cleaver and you will never regret it. I prefer a cleaver that weighs about 8 ounces and is 3 inches wide by 8 inches long. If you can't find what you're looking for in stores, try the Internet (www.knife.com).

Handling your cleaver is not difficult. Grasp the handle of the cleaver close to the blade with your left or right hand. Extend and place your index finger along one side of the blade and your thumb on the other. Using your other hand, firmly hold in place the item to be cut. Knuckles are extended to lightly touch the flat of the blade and act as a cutting guide. The cutting edge should never be lifted above the knuckles. The blade cuts in short, shallow strokes. Move it forward and down.

Sharpening the cleaver is also very important. To restore a razor's edge, use a few strokes of a sharpening rod at a 15-degree angle. Every couple of months, use a whetstone at a 10-degree angle to keep the edge sharp. Do not use an electric sharpener.

Treat your cleaver as you would any fine piece of cutlery. Always wash your cleaver by hand, never in the dishwasher. Don't let it sit in water for long periods of time. Dry the cleaver before putting it away. It's best to store the cleaver in a wooden block, or against a magnetic strip. If you must store it in a drawer, lay it flat with the blade away from other knives.

Cutting board

All her life my mother used a round Chinese chopping block 15 inches in diameter, 6 inches thick, and cut from a hardwood tree trunk. If you'd like to use an old-fashioned cutting board, you might be able to find one at an Asian store. I prefer to use a high-density polyethylene cutting board. It is acid resistant; will not chip, peel, crack, or warp; is easy to clean; and is dishwasher safe. Since both sides can be used, I use one side for meat and the other side for vegetables. I don't recommend cutting boards with suction cups on the underside. These boards are susceptible to damage when using your cleaver to crush food, and only one side of the board can be used. Be sure to choose a cutting board large enough to hold 2 to 3 cups of ingredients.

Spatula/ladle

The ladle is curved while the Chinese spatula is flat. Restaurant chefs use both a ladle and a spatula to stir food. With the oil and condiments right in front of them, chefs employ the ladle both as a stirrer and as a measuring and transferring device. At home I like to use two spatulas to stir-fry, lifting and dropping as if tossing a salad. If you use a Dutch oven, you can use two wooden spoons to stir with a circular motion.

Wire skimmer

Made of copper-wire mesh and varying in size from 6 inches to 10 inches in diameter, the skimmer is very handy for turning ingredients in hot oil or for removing vegetables from hot water after blanching. It is no longer used just for Chinese cooking. I use it even when I cook soft- or hard-boiled eggs.

Rice cooker

For most Chinese people, the rice cooker is as important as the wok. Since most Chinese kitchen stoves have just two burners, rice cookers are popular because they don't occupy a burner. Even if you have a large kitchen, a rice cooker is a good investment. It produces perfect rice every time, never undercooked or overcooked. It can also be used as a steamer when you need to steam food for a short period of time.

Chopsticks

When I was four years old, my mother told me that the Chinese are civilized people because we use a pair of chopsticks to pick up our food, unlike Westerners who use forks and knives. She said Westerners were barbarians! Of course, I never dreamed that two decades later I would be married to a Westerner. I still use chopsticks just about every day to eat and to cook.

There are many different kinds of chopsticks: gold, silver, ivory, lacquered wood, jade, polished bone, plain bamboo. The bamboo ones are the cheapest and most practical. They're about 10 inches long, with ¼-inch-square thickness at the top, and the bottom half rounded and lightly tapered. Use the round ends to pick up and carry food to your month. Chinese people usually keep the square top of chopsticks clean to serve food to others.

In China, rice is served in a rice bowl, and it is quite common to use chopsticks to push the rice directly into the mouth from the bowl. Even I find it difficult to eat rice from a plate with chopsticks and will often use a fork instead. When I was a child, my mother taught me that when I finished eating, the chopsticks should be placed together on top of the rice bowl, pointing away from me, thus indicating to other members of the family and to guests that they should continue enjoying their food.

You should never place your chopsticks upright in your rice. To many Chinese people, this symbolizes death because it resembles incense burning upright in remembrance of the dead.

If you've never used chopsticks before, here's what to do:

1. Put one chopstick between the palm and the base of the thumb, using the ring finger (the fourth finger) to support the lower part of the chopstick. With the thumb, squeeze the chopstick down while the ring finger pushes it up. The chopstick should be stationary and very stable.
2. Use the tips of the thumb, index, and middle fingers to hold the other chopstick like a pen. Make sure the tips of the two chopsticks line up.
3. Pivot the upper chopstick up and down towards the stationary lower chopstick. With this motion you can pick up anything!

It takes a little practice to master using chopsticks. Don't be discouraged. Once you learn the skill, I guarantee that you will enjoy eating Chinese food even more.

Chinese rolling pin

A Chinese rolling pin is indispensable when making dim sum, such as Pot Stickers and Roast Pork Steamed Buns. It is a dowel-like wooden roller about 1 inch in diameter and 12 inches long. In my cooking classes, I always point out to my students that I have one rolling pin that I've used for more than thirty years. I consider this rolling pin to be my best friend. You should never soak your rolling pin in water. Wash it with mild soap, rinse, and dry thoroughly.

Cutting methods

Since Chinese people eat exclusively with chopsticks, food has to be precut into bite-sized pieces. Ingredients should be cut uniformly for even cooking and nicer presentation. Meat and poultry should be cut across the grain to enhance tenderness. If you are not used to handling a Chinese cleaver, a chef's knife is a good substitute. Cooking Chinese food is really a labor of love; ninety percent of the preparation involves cutting.

My mother taught me at a very young age that there is a trick to cutting. Place a wet cloth under your cutting board to keep it stable. A stable board makes cutting much easier. Freezing the meat slightly will also make cutting easier.

There are several cutting techniques in Chinese cooking:

- **Slicing:** Cut food into pieces that are $\frac{1}{8}$ to $\frac{1}{4}$ inch thick by $1\frac{1}{2}$ to 2 inches long.
- **Shredding:** Gather together food that has been sliced, as described above, then cut again into $\frac{1}{4}$-inch pieces.
- **Dicing:** Cut food into cubes that are about $\frac{1}{2}$ inch in size.
- **Cubing:** Similar to dicing, except the cubes are up to 1 inch in size.
- **Mincing:** Cut food into $\frac{1}{16}$-inch-square pieces or smaller.
- **Rolling cut:** A technique for cutting long, round items such as asparagus, carrots, and potatoes into uniform pieces. Turn the item to be cut with one hand while the other hand holds the cleaver and cuts the item diagonally. Change the angle of the cleaver as necessary to insure even-sized pieces.

To learn more about cutting techniques, see the section on the Chinese cleaver earlier in this chapter.

How to de-bone a chicken

1. Rinse a fresh chicken with tap water and dry well with paper towels. A frozen chicken should be completely thawed, rinsed, and dried in the same manner.
2. Place the chicken breast side down, butt end away from you. With a cleaver or sharp knife, cut a ¼-inch-deep slice along the spine of the back.
3. Stand the chicken on its butt end, with the breast side facing you. Pull back the skin and find the joint that attaches the wing to the breast. (There should be a distinct dent where the small drumstick joins the breast.) Cut a slot ½ inch deep close to the breast side. With one hand holding the breastbone, pull the wing off the chicken. The skin and part of the breast will come off at the same time. Remove the other wing in the same way.
4. Place the chicken on its back, breast side up, with the butt end toward you. Cut each thigh from the chicken.
5. Take each thigh and cut the drumstick section off at the joint. Cut the drumstick open to remove the meat. Scrape away gristle, fat, and any small bones.
6. Hold the thigh by the joint which had been attached to the body of the chicken. Slowly scrape down the bone with a cleaver to remove the meat in one piece. Cut away fat and gristle. Repeat the process for the other thigh.
7. Cut or scrape the breast filet from the breastbone, getting as close to the bone as possible.
8. To remove gristle from the breast filet, hold the gristle with one hand and, with a cleaver or sharp knife in your other hand, scrape the meat away from you using short, quick strokes.
9. Take each detached wing and cut the breast meat away from the wing joint. Save the wings for soup stock or other use.
10. You now have boneless chicken meat, but before it is ready to be used for various stir-fried dishes, you must remove all remaining fat and skin.
11. Save the carcass, skin, and bones to make soup stock. Discard all fat.

How to bone a duck

(To "bone" means to remove the bone while leaving the meat behind.)

1. If the duck is frozen, thaw completely. Remove loose fat from areas around the neck and tail.
2. Pull the skin away from the neck to expose the breastbone and wing joints.
3. Cut through the breastbone and wing joints with a paring knife or sharp scissors.
4. Cut the meat along the bones, using small snips. Pull the bones from the carcass, leaving the meat behind.
5. Continue until you reach the thighbones. Disjoint each thighbone from the backbone, then free the drumstick from the backbone. Leave the tailbone, with the flesh and skin attached.

This method can be used to bone other whole fowl.

Chinese Cooking Methods

The terminology of Chinese cooking is quite complicated, and for some methods there are no English words to describe them. The following are the most common methods for preparing Chinese food:

COOKING IN OIL

Stir-frying 炒

This is a uniquely Chinese cooking method called chao 炒. Ingredients are fried with constant stirring until cooking is completed, usually within a few minutes. Use a very small amount of oil in very high heat (about 375 degrees or higher). Remember, always heat your wok or pan to the smoking point, then add the oil to prevent sticking and to seal in the juices (unless you are using a nonstick wok). Butter cannot be used since it will burn when cooking with high heat. Olive oil has too strong a flavor and is foreign to Chinese tastes. Sesame oil, with its strong aroma, is used chiefly as a flavoring. Peanut oil, vegetable oil, soybean oil, and canola oil are able to tolerate high heat without smoking.

Stir-frying is widely used throughout China, but is most popular in southern cooking. Since stir-frying requires quick cooking over high heat, I recommend that you cook no more than one pound of meat and one pound of vegetables at a time. A home range usually is not powerful enough to provide the high heat required for stir-frying a larger amount.

All ingredients in the same dish should be of even size (slicing, dicing, shredding, or mincing) and shape. Meat and vegetables are usually cooked separately. Vegetables such as broccoli, asparagus, snow peas, and sugar peas can be parboiled before stir-frying. Meat and poultry should be marinated; ginger, garlic, and green onions minced; and seasoning sauce prepared in advance. It is important to have all ingredients prepared and placed within easy reach of the stove. Always cook and serve your stir-fried dish as your last dish. That way, the cooked vegetables will be crispy and crunchy.

Pan-frying 煎

Pan-frying is best done with a flat, 8- to 10-inch frying pan, using a small amount of oil over low heat. Food is cooked slowly until it is crispy brown outside and tender inside. This method is commonly used in all regions of China.

Deep-frying 炸

Food can be deep-fried at different temperatures: high heat (375 degrees or higher), medium heat (about 350 degrees), or low heat (250 to 300 degrees). Deep-frying is especially popular in the eastern and western regions of China. Many dishes, such as General Tso's Chicken and Crispy Beef, are deep-fried in medium-heat oil, then deep-fried again in high-heat oil to yield a crispy outside and tender cooked inside. I reuse deep-fried oil that has been strained through a coffee filter and refrigerated.

COOKING IN LIQUID

Stocks 上湯

My mother used two kinds of soup bases: chicken stock 雞湯 and meat stock 肉湯. Fujian 福建, a southern coastal province of China and my parents' birthplace, is famous for its stocks, soups, and soupy dishes. You can learn how to make chicken stock on page 18, in the chapter on soups. I recommend using homemade chicken stock for soup dishes. For most other dishes, you can substitute canned chicken stock. Meat stock is made from pork or pork bone using the same method as when making chicken stock. Meat stock has a great deal of transparent fat on top, which must be removed. You can refrigerate chicken stock and meat stock, then remove the fat when it solidifies. Stocks keep about four or five days in the refrigerator and for months in the freezer. They are rich and flavorful and superb ingredients for hearty soups.

Red cooking 紅燒

Red cooking is similar to American stewing, except that it requires large quantities of dark soy sauce, and such spices as star anise, Sichuan peppercorns, ginger, garlic, and green onions. Dark soy sauce makes dishes rich and reddish and is usually used in preparing pork, beef, chicken, or duck. The cooking time can range from one to three hours. Red-cooked dishes can be served hot or cold. They can be reheated in the microwave and served again at any time.

Braising 燉

First sear the food in hot oil, then simmer it with seasoning sauce in a covered wok or skillet. The result is food that is rich and flavorful.

Steaming 蒸

When food is steamed, it usually presents the best of its natural flavors. You don't have to add oil or seasoning during the cooking process, so the food is neither oily nor greasy. Learn more about steaming on page 9, in the preceding chapter on utensils and cutting.

COOKING OVER FIRE

Roasting and barbecuing 烤

Although Peking Duck is famous around the world, roasting and barbecuing are not common practices in China. Since most Chinese kitchens don't have ovens, these methods have never been integrated into home cooking. Often, Chinese people simply buy this type of prepared food from restaurants or specialty food stores. Nowadays, with American kitchens equipped with all types of modern cooking appliances, roasting and barbecuing can easily be done at home.

Smoking 燻

Smoking is a popular method for flavoring food. Poultry and fish are precooked and smoked over rice, tea, and brown sugar. Smoking gives the food deep color and a special flavor.

COLD MIXING 涼拌

This method consists of cut-up food or parboiled vegetables mixed with a dressing and served like an American salad. Most dressings contain ingredients such as soy sauce, vinegar, sugar, and sesame oil. Cold mixing is a wonderful way to prepare one dish ahead of time.

SERVING CHINESE FOOD

I come from a family of seven people, and I have one brother and three sisters. My mother always prepared three dishes and a soup for lunch and dinner, and we always sat at a round table. Our meal consisted of one pork dish, mostly cooked with vegetables, one whole fish dish, and one vegetable or tofu dish. Chinese people eat rice like Westerners eat bread, pasta, or potatoes. Rice is a very important part of a daily meal. For the majority of Chinese people, a daily meal consists of something to go with a bowl of rice rather than a few tablespoons of rice along with a big serving of fish or meat. Chinese people drink tea all day long but almost never with meals. There is one exception: tea is served with dim sum.

In China, a wedding banquet or birthday party is a very elaborate ceremony. Ten to twelve people usually sit at a large round table, and ten to twelve dishes are served. The dishes consist of a variety of cold cuts, pork, beef, duck, chicken, fish, shrimp, noodles, tofu, two kinds of soup, plain boiled rice, and two kinds of dessert.

I love to entertain friends, but I usually invite only two couples for a dinner party. Thus, counting my husband and myself, I normally prepare a six-course meal for six people. I have a unique way of serving my guests Chinese food the American way. I serve hot soup in the winter as a first course, or as an appetizer. In the summer, I serve a salad following an appetizer. Two main courses follow: one is stir-fried; the other could be steamed, smoked, roasted, red-cooked, or braised. On most occasions I serve either plain boiled rice, fried rice, or curried rice. Chinese hosts usually do not serve dessert after a meal, only fresh fruit. Over the years I've become Americanized and usually serve my guests a light dessert.

When I prepare Chinese food for my husband and myself, I usually serve one meat, seafood, or chicken dish with vegetables and rice. The recipes in this book usually are designed for three to four people, which explains why I always manage to have enough food for two nights. If you have four people in your family, one dish with rice is sufficient. If cooking for more than four people, you may wish to consider preparing a second dish.

Remember, Chinese cooking is really quite easy as long as you have the right utensils and ingredients and are willing to practice. You will soon discover the rich variety of Chinese cooking and quickly master the techniques. Good luck and good eating!

Soups

CHICKEN STOCK
雞湯

Students often ask me, "What is the difference between chicken stock and chicken broth?" When you make soup with meat and bones, you produce chicken broth. When you make soup with bones only, you produce chicken stock. To create a tasty soup, you have to start with good broth or stock. Since we never drink beverages at the table in China, soups are an essential part of almost every Chinese meal. Stocks keep about four or five days in the refrigerator and for months in the freezer.

INGREDIENTS
4 pounds chicken with bones
   or 6 pounds chicken bones only
4 slices ginger, smashed
1 whole green onion, smashed
3 to 4 quarts cold water

Remove the fat and skin from the chicken. Cut up the chicken to separate the wings, breast, thighs, legs, and back. Wash the chicken parts. Put the cut-up chicken into a large soup pot, with enough water to cover it. Bring to a rapid boil. Discard the water and rinse the chicken well. Put the blanched chicken into the soup pot. Add ginger, green onion, and water. Bring to a boil again, cover, turn down the heat to very low, and simmer for 2 to 3 hours.

Let cool. Slowly and gently pour out the stock into a very fine mesh strainer, then discard the chicken. Put the stock into a refrigerator overnight. The next day, remove most of the solidified fat from the stock, but leave some to give the stock flavor. A little fat makes a stock smooth, mellow, and fragrant.

Note: For most of the recipes in this cookbook (except for the soup recipes) requiring the use of chicken stock, I use the canned variety. If you prefer to make your own chicken stock, add salt to your taste when you cook soups or any other dishes.

EGG DROP SOUP
蛋花湯

This is such a simple dish that even a child can make it. It tastes better if you use a very rich homemade chicken stock instead of canned stock. If you do use canned stock, omit the salt. I sometimes use only egg yolks to make this soup. If you like dried seaweed, shred it and sprinkle on top.

INGREDIENTS
2 eggs, well beaten
2 teaspoons vegetable oil or sesame oil
6 cups chicken stock (see page 18)
2 teaspoons salt
4 tablespoons cornstarch and 4 tablespoons water to make a paste
1 whole green onion, minced

Beat eggs well, but not until frothy. Blend in the oil, mix well, and set aside. Mix cornstarch with water. Mince green onion.

Over high heat, bring the chicken stock to a boil. Add salt. Turn heat to low and slowly stir in cornstarch paste until the stock lightly thickens. Slowly pour in the beaten eggs while stirring. Remove from heat instantly. Garnish with green onion.

Serves 6 to 7.

HOT AND SOUR SOUP
酸辣湯

This soup is actually considered a dish for country people, since the cost of the ingredients is very reasonable. The authentic way to prepare this dish is to add steamed and jellied chicken blood, but I choose to delete this ingredient. I enjoy this soup even more the next day.

INGREDIENTS

¼ pound boneless pork
1 tub (16 ounces) firm or soft tofu
2 tablespoons dried wood ears, shredded
½ cup bamboo shoots, shredded
2 eggs, well beaten
¼ cup cornstarch and ¼ cup water to make a paste
6 cups chicken stock (see page 18)
1 teaspoon salt
1 whole green onion, minced
Dash of red pepper powder or chili oil (optional)

SEASONING SAUCE

3 tablespoons soy sauce
3 tablespoons rice vinegar
1 teaspoon sesame oil
¼ teaspoon black pepper

MARINADE

1 teaspoon soy sauce
½ teaspoon cornstarch
½ teaspoon sesame oil

In a bowl, mix marinade. Cut the pork with the grain into ⅛-inch-thick slices, then cut against the grain into 2-inch-long shreds and marinate for 20 to 30 minutes. Soak the wood ears in warm water in a small bowl for 20 minutes. Wash the wood ears, drain, and cut into shreds. Shred bamboo shoots and tofu. Beat eggs in a small bowl. Mix cornstarch and water in another bowl to make a paste. In a small bowl, combine seasoning sauce.

Pour chicken stock into a deep pot and bring to a boil over high heat. Add salt. Add pork and stir to separate the pork shreds. Cook about 1 minute. Add tofu, bamboo shoots, and wood ears, and bring to boil again. Turn heat to low and slowly stir in cornstarch paste until soup thickens. Turn heat even lower and add seasoning sauce. Slow pour in the beaten eggs while stirring. Sprinkle with minced green onion. Serve with red pepper powder or chili oil if desired.

Serves 6 to 7.

MEATBALLS AND WINTER MELON SOUP
冬瓜肉圓湯

In China there is a very fancy and famous soup that is served only at a formal banquet. The soup contains a whole melon that is hand carved in a very elaborate design that can take days to accomplish. It is truly a work of art. My mother served the following simple and economical version of this soup quite often, since we had two meals a day and soup was a must on the table.

INGREDIENTS
½ pound ground pork
2 packages (1.3 ounces each) cellophane
    noodles
1½ pounds cut up winter melon, sliced
6 cups chicken stock (see page 18)
2 teaspoons salt
1 whole green onion, chopped

MARINADE
1 tablespoon soy sauce
1 teaspoon rice wine
2 teaspoons cornstarch
1 tablespoon water
1 teaspoon ginger, minced

In a bowl, mix marinade. Marinate pork for 20 to 30 minutes. Soak cellophane noodles in hot water until soft (about 10 to 12 minutes), then cut into shorter lengths (6 to 8 inches). Rinse and drain. Peel the green skin off the melon. Discard the seeds and cut out the soft part next to the seeds. Wash and pat dry with paper towels. Cut into ¼-inch-thick by 2-inch-long slices.

Bring the chicken stock to a boil over high heat. Add salt and sliced winter melon. Heat until the stock boils again. Turn heat to low and cook for 20 to 30 minutes.

In another pot, bring 4 cups of water to a boil. Form the pork mixture into meatballs by using a small ice cream scoop, or by grabbing a fistful of pork mixture in one hand, squeezing it up through a curled index finger, and scooping it off with a wet spoon. Drop the meatballs in the boiling water one by one until the pork mixture is finished. Cook for 3 minutes and drain.

When the winter melon soup is simmering, add the meatballs the last 10 minutes and the cellophane noodles the last 5 minutes. Sprinkle with green onion.

Serves 4 to 5.

MINCED CHICKEN WITH CORN SOUP
雞茸粟米湯

Spanish and Portuguese explorers brought corn to China more than 400 years ago. This soup, served at our wedding rehearsal, was one that my husband and I selected. In fact, it was the first time that he had tasted this classic soup. It has since become a family favorite. In my cooking class, I usually double this recipe, one using fresh corn and the other canned corn. The majority of my students prefer this soup made from canned creamed corn.

INGREDIENTS
½ pound boneless and skinless chicken breasts
1 large can (15 ounces) cream-style sweet corn
   or 2 large fresh ears of corn, shucked
4 egg whites
6 cups chicken stock (see page 18)
2 teaspoons salt
4 tablespoons cornstarch and 4 tablespoons water to make a paste
½ cup ham, minced

With a cleaver or sharp knife, slice the kernels of fresh corn from their cobs. Mince chicken breast into fine slivers and set aside. Beat 4 egg whites lightly and mince the ham. Mix cornstarch with water to make a paste and set aside.

Have the minced chicken, creamed corn or fresh corn, beaten egg whites, chicken stock, cornstarch paste, and minced ham within easy reach. Pour chicken stock into a deep pot. Add chicken, corn, and salt, and bring to a boil over high heat. Stir the soup mixture often until it boils. Turn heat to low and slowly stir in cornstarch paste until the soup thickens. Slowly pour in the beaten egg whites while stirring. Pour into a hot bowl or a soup tureen and sprinkle with minced ham. Sprinkle with fresh ground black pepper if desired.

Serves 6 to 7.

SHRIMP SOUP WITH CRISPY RICE
鍋巴蝦仁湯

For years when I taught this dish, my students were crazy about it. Since ready-made crispy rice (guo ba) wasn't available in Asian supermarkets in those days, crispy rice had to be prepared by hand and deep-fried. Nowadays, you can buy ready-made guo ba, either already deep-fried or unfried. If you buy the deep-fried kind, no further preparation is necessary. To prepare unfried guo ba, heat 2 cups of oil to 375 degrees and deep-fry the pieces until they become puffed and golden brown.

INGREDIENTS
10 ounces medium shrimp
5 ounces lean pork
4 ounces snow peas
5 dried Chinese mushrooms, shredded
6 pieces of ready-made crispy rice or
    homemade crispy rice (see page 128)
6 tablespoons oil for cooking shrimp and
    pork
6 cups chicken stock (see page 18)
1 teaspoon salt

MARINADE FOR SHRIMP
1 teaspoon rice wine
1 teaspoon cornstarch
½ teaspoon salt

SEASONING SAUCE
2 tablespoons soy sauce
½ teaspoon white pepper
2 teaspoons sugar
1 tablespoon rice vinegar
2 tablespoons rice wine
1 tablespoon sesame oil
¼ cup cornstarch and ¼ cup water to make
    a paste

MARINADE FOR PORK
1 teaspoon soy sauce
1 teaspoon cornstarch

Preheat oven to 400 degrees. In a bowl, mix shrimp marinade. Wash shrimp if desired. Shell shrimp and remove the black vein. Dry with paper towels and marinate for 20 to 30 minutes. In another bowl, mix pork marinade. Cut the pork with the grain into ⅛-inch-thick slices, then cut against the grain into shreds 1½ to 2 inches long. Marinate for 20 to 30 minutes.

Soak mushrooms in hot water for 20 minutes. Discard the water and squeeze the mushrooms dry. Cut off and discard mushroom stems, then cut each cap into ¼-inch strips. Bring 2 cups of water to a boil. Add snow peas (break off tips and remove strings) and parboil about 30 seconds. Remove and drain. In a small bowl, combine seasoning sauce. Put 6 pieces of crispy rice on a cookie sheet and bake for 10 minutes until hot.

Heat a wok or large skillet over high heat until hot; add 6 tablespoons of oil and heat until hot. Stir-fry shrimp and pork for 2 minutes. Remove and drain. Leave 1 tablespoon of oil in wok and stir-fry mushrooms for 1 minute. Add chicken stock and bring to a boil. Add shrimp, pork, parboiled snow peas, and salt into the soup stock. Bring the stock to a boil again. Turn heat to low and stir in seasoning sauce until the soup thickens. Remove to a soup tureen. Quickly take the crispy rice to the table and place in individual soup bowls. Add the soup mixture over each. Serve immediately.

Serves 5 to 6.

SPINACH AND TOFU SOUP
菠菜豆腐湯

My memories go as far back as when I was in playschool. My mother often told me that spinach and tofu were healthy foods, so this dish was served quite often at our dining table. Nowadays I eat lots of spinach and tofu. This soup is really a very pretty one, with jade green from the spinach, pure white from the tofu, and pink from the ham. It is an ideal soup to serve on a winter day.

INGREDIENTS
10 ounces fresh spinach
1 tub (16 ounces) firm or soft tofu
½ pound boneless and skinless chicken
    breasts
6 dried Chinese mushrooms, shredded
2 tablespoons oil
6 cups chicken stock (see page 18)
2 teaspoons salt
4 tablespoons cornstarch and 4 tablespoons
    water to make a paste
2 eggs, well beaten with 2 teaspoons sesame
    oil
¼ cup ham, minced

MARINADE
1 teaspoon soy sauce
1 teaspoon sesame oil
1 teaspoon cornstarch

Wash the spinach well, then drain. Cut the spinach into small pieces. Set aside. In a bowl, mix marinade. Cut the tofu into thin slices. Slice chicken against the grain into ⅛-inch slices and marinate for 20 to 30 minutes. Soak mushrooms in hot water for 20 minutes. Discard the water and squeeze the mushrooms dry. Cut off and discard mushroom stems, then cut each cap into ¼-inch strips.

Heat a wok or large skillet over high heat until hot; add oil and heat until hot. Add the chicken and stir-fry until the pieces are white and firm (about 2 minutes). Remove to a small plate.

Pour chicken stock into a deep pot and bring to a boil over high heat. Add mushrooms, salt, tofu, and chicken. When mixture boils again, slowly stir in cornstarch paste until the soup thickens. Add the spinach and cook for 30 seconds. Slowly pour in the egg and sesame oil mixture while stirring. Remove from heat instantly. Pour into a hot bowl and sprinkle with minced ham. Sprinkle with fresh ground black pepper if desired.

Serves 6 to 7.

TOFU WITH CRABMEAT SOUP
蟹肉豆腐湯

This is quite a tasty soup, but you must use the best quality crabmeat. Other kinds of vegetables can be substituted for spinach, such as asparagus, arugula, bok choy, or any leafy vegetable. If you don't like tofu, you can use just crabmeat and vegetables.

INGREDIENTS
1 tub (16 ounces) firm or soft tofu
8 ounces cooked crabmeat
4 ounces fresh spinach
6 cups chicken stock (see page 18)
2 teaspoons ginger juice (see page 165)
2 teaspoons salt
4 to 6 tablespoons cornstarch and 4 to 6 tablespoons water to make a paste
3 egg whites, beaten
4 tablespoons minced ham
  or 4 tablespoons chopped green onions

Wash the spinach well, then drain. Cut the spinach into small pieces. Set aside. Cut the tofu into thin slices. Pour chicken stock into a deep pot and bring to a boil over high heat. Add crabmeat, tofu, ginger juice, and salt. When mixture boils again, turn heat to low and slowly stir in cornstarch paste until the soup thickens. Add the spinach and slowly pour in the beaten egg whites while stirring. Remove from heat instantly. Pour into a hot bowl and sprinkle with minced ham or chopped green onions. Sprinkle with fresh ground black pepper if desired.

Serves 6 to 7.

WONTON SOUP
餛飩湯

This soup actually is considered a dim sum, but I often serve it to my family and guests as a first course. When I was a poor college student in Taiwan in the early 1960s, my roommate Helena and I would order wonton soup from a street vendor after late-night studies in the library. The soup contained mostly noodles and only two or three wontons. In the classroom nowadays, I often brag to my students that I am so rich that I can have ten wontons just for lunch! I recommend making lots of wontons at one time. This recipe makes 70 to 80 wontons; select 2 to 3 dozen for the soup and freeze the remainder.

FILLING
1 pound ground pork
1 egg, well beaten
2 tablespoons green onion, minced
1 teaspoon ginger, minced
1 tablespoon sesame oil
1 teaspoon salt
2 teaspoons cornstarch
1 tablespoon rice wine
2 tablespoons soy sauce
3 to 4 tablespoons water

OTHER INGREDIENTS
Wonton wrappers (skins)
4 cups chicken stock (see page 18)
1 tablespoon soy sauce
1 teaspoon salt
2 to 3 cups leafy vegetable, torn coarsely
4 tablespoons green onion, chopped
Few drops chili oil or chili sauce (optional)

Mix the filling ingredients in a large bowl, being sure to add the water 1 tablespoon at a time. Mix until smooth. Set aside until ready to use. Put 1 teaspoon of filling in the center of each square of wonton skin and fold corner to corner to make a triangle. Pinch together the widest two outer corners with water.

Makes 70 to 80 wontons.

In a 4- to 5-quart saucepan, bring 2 quarts of water to a boil and drop in the wontons. Cover and bring to a boil. As soon as the water boils, add 1 cup of cold water. When the water boils again, remove saucepan from heat and let the wontons remain in the water for 5 minutes with the cover on. Scoop out the wontons using a skimmer.

Pour the chicken stock into a medium-sized saucepan and bring to a boil. Add soy sauce, salt, and vegetables and cook for 1 minute. Set aside. Put wontons in individual bowls or in a large serving bowl. Pour the hot stock and vegetables over the wontons and garnish with green onion (adding a few drops of chili oil or chili sauce if desired). Serve immediately.

Serves 3 to 4.

Pork

CHINESE ROAST PORK
叉燒肉

When I was a youngster in Tainan, we didn't have an oven in our home. On special occasions, my mother would go to the grocery store to buy ready-made roast pork. Nowadays in the United States you can still find roast pork hanging in Chinese markets for people to purchase. Some people want it simply to accompany their drinks. Others use it for making steamed buns, lo mein, fried rice, roast pork with almonds, etc.

INGREDIENTS
1½ pounds pork tenderloin or pork loin
2 tablespoons honey
1 tablespoon sesame oil (optional)
Hoisin sauce for dipping (optional)
Lettuce leaves (optional)
Shredded green onions (optional)

MARINADE
¼ cup hoisin sauce
¼ cup sugar
¼ cup dark soy sauce
2 tablespoons rice wine
½ teaspoon five-spice powder
1 tablespoon garlic, minced
1 tablespoon ginger, minced
2 whole green onions, minced
1 teaspoon red food coloring (optional)

Preheat oven to 350 degrees. Cut the pork into 9-inch x 1½-inch strips. In a bowl, mix marinade. Marinate the pork and leave in the refrigerator for at least 2 hours, turning over several times.

Place pork strips in a roasting pan and bake on a greased rack for 1 hour. Keep the pork strips moist by putting 1 inch of water in the pan. Baste once using leftover marinade, turn pork over, and baste other side. Remove the pork from the oven and increase the temperature to 400 degrees. Brush the pork with honey and bake for an additional 4 minutes on each side. Take the meat out and brush with sesame oil if desired. Slice the pork and serve hot or cold. Serve hoisin sauce as a dip if desired.

You can also spread 1 teaspoon of hoisin sauce on a lettuce leaf with shredded green onions and several slices of pork. Roll up the lettuce leaf and serve.

As main course, serves 2 to 3.
As appetizer, serves 7 to 8.

Diced Chinese Roast Pork with Almonds
杏仁叉燒丁

Since my family never owned an oven when we lived in Taiwan, roast pork had to be bought in a restaurant or at a market. When my mother made this dish, it was a really special treat for all of us. Since American kitchens have ovens, preparing this dish is easy and convenient. In fact, when you have leftover American-style roast beef or roast pork, you can substitute it for the Chinese roast pork in this recipe.

INGREDIENTS

1 pound cooked Chinese roast pork
1 cup celery, diced
1 cup carrots, diced
1 cup water chestnuts or bamboo shoots, diced
3 tablespoons oil
2 teaspoons ginger, minced
2 teaspoons garlic, minced
½ teaspoon salt
½ cup chicken stock
½ cup toasted almond slivers

SEASONING SAUCE

2 tablespoons soy sauce
2 tablespoons oyster sauce
1 tablespoon sesame oil
1 teaspoon sugar
2 tablespoons rice wine
1 tablespoon cornstarch and 1 tablespoon water to make a paste

Cut pork with the grain into ¼-inch slices. Then cut again with the grain into ¼-inch strips. Put the strips together and cut across the grain into ¼-inch dice. Dice celery, carrots, and water chestnuts (or bamboo shoots) into ¼-inch pieces. Mince ginger and garlic. In a small bowl, combine seasoning sauce.

Heat a wok or large skillet over high heat until hot; add oil and heat until hot. Stir-fry the ginger and garlic for about 20 seconds. Add pork, vegetables, salt, and chicken stock. Cover and cook over high heat for about 2 minutes. Add seasoning sauce and stir well until the meat and vegetables are coated with sauce. Pour into a serving platter. Sprinkle with almonds.

Serves 3 to 4.

DOUBLE-COOKED PORK
回鍋肉

This dish is another famous Sichuan specialty known worldwide. Once when my husband and I were in Scotland in the early 1990s, we enjoyed this spicy food in a small Chinese restaurant in Glasgow. In China, when we talk of eating meat, it is understood that we mean pork meat. This dish's name in Chinese literally means "return to wok meat," reflecting the fact that the pork is cooked twice, the second time in a wok.

INGREDIENTS
1 pound boneless pork in 1 piece
   (preferably center-cut boneless pork)
1 tablespoon rice wine
1 slice ginger, smashed
1 whole green onion, smashed
2 to 3 medium sweet peppers
   or 3 to 4 cups cut-up green cabbage
3 to 4 tablespoons oil
1 tablespoon garlic, minced

SEASONING SAUCE
¼ cup sweet bean sauce
2 tablespoons hot bean sauce
1 tablespoon sugar
2 tablespoons rice wine
2 tablespoons water
½ to 1 teaspoon chili oil

Cut the pork into 9-inch x 1½-inch strips. Put the pork in a pot with enough water to cover. Bring to a boil with rice wine, ginger, and onion. Turn heat to medium-low to maintain a strong simmer, cover, and cook for 25 minutes. Remove pork from water and let cool. After pork has cooled, cut into ⅛-inch slices when you are ready to stir-fry them. Seed and cut the peppers (or cut-up cabbage) into pieces approximating the size and shape of the meat (use rolling cut). In a small bowl, combine seasoning sauce.

Heat a wok or large skillet over high heat until hot; add oil and heat until hot. Toss in the garlic and peppers (or cabbage) and stir rapidly for about 1 to 2 minutes. Add the pork slices to the vegetable mixture and cook for another minute. Pour in the seasoning sauce. Stir in fast, folding motions until the contents are well coated by the sauce.

Serves 3 to 4.

LION'S HEAD
獅子頭

This is a very famous dish from Yangzhou, Jiangsu Province. The large meatballs are thought to represent the heads of lions, and the cabbage represents their manes. Lion's Head is perfect for a buffet dinner and is essentially a trouble-free dish to make. It can be cooked one day in advance and then reheated in the microwave. Plain boiled rice goes well with this dish.

INGREDIENTS

1 pound ground pork or ground beef
5 water chestnuts, chopped
1 pound napa cabbage
1 tablespoon oil
2 tablespoons cornstarch and 2 tablespoons
   water to make a paste
1 tablespoon soy sauce
1 teaspoon sugar
½ cup chicken stock

MARINADE

1 egg, well beaten
1 teaspoon ginger, minced
2 tablespoons cornstarch
1 tablespoon rice wine
2 tablespoons soy sauce
⅛ teaspoon black pepper
2 tablespoons water
2 tablespoons green onion, minced

In a medium bowl, combine the meat and the marinade with your hand or an electric mixer until smooth; set aside for 15 minutes. Add the water chestnuts and shape the mixture into 4 meatballs. Wash the cabbage and cut off the root end, then cut the leaves and stems into 2-inch sections.

Heat a wok or large skillet over medium-high heat until hot; add oil and heat until hot. Dip the meatballs in cornstarch paste one at a time. Fry the meatballs until all sides are golden brown. Remove the meatballs to a plate. Stir-fry the cabbage in the same wok or skillet for 1 minute. Add soy sauce, sugar, and chicken stock and cook another 45 seconds.

Place half of the cooked cabbage in an ovenproof casserole with meatballs on top and pour the remaining cabbage with juice over the meatballs. Bake in a preheated 275-degree oven for 1 hour or simmer 1 hour on the stove. Serve directly from the casserole.

Serves 3 to 4.

MOO SHI PORK
木須肉

Moo shi in Chinese means yellow cassia blossoms. When scrambled eggs are cooked and cut into small pieces, they resemble the yellow blossoms of this shrub. This is a northern dish and is usually served with Mandarin pancakes. Nowadays, it's common to brush hoisin sauce on the pancake first, then place about 2 tablespoons of moo shi pork on top. Just roll up the pancake and eat!

INGREDIENTS
½ pound lean pork
2 tablespoons dried wood ears, shredded
20 pieces dried tiger lily stems
1 tablespoon dried shrimp, minced
1 cup bamboo shoots, shredded
1 cup green cabbage, shredded
3 whole green onions, shredded
5 tablespoons oil
1 teaspoon ginger, minced
3 eggs, well beaten (add dash of salt)
Mandarin pancakes (optional, see page 136)
Hoisin sauce (optional)

SEASONING SAUCE
2 tablespoons oyster sauce
1 teaspoon soy sauce
1 tablespoon rice wine
¼ cup chicken stock
2 teaspoons cornstarch with 2 teaspoons
   water to make a paste
1 teaspoon sesame oil

MARINADE
2 teaspoons rice wine
½ tablespoon soy sauce
1 teaspoon cornstarch

In a bowl, mix marinade. Cut the pork with the grain into ⅛-inch-thick slices, then cut against the grain into 2-inch-long shreds and marinate for 20 to 30 minutes. Soak wood ears, tiger lily stems, and shrimp in separate bowls of hot water for 20 minutes. Clean, rinse, and shred wood ears. Bunch tiger lily stems together, then cut into 1½-inch sections. Mince dried shrimp. Set all these ingredients on a large plate. Shred bamboo shoots, cabbage, and green onions and add to ingredients on the same plate. In a small bowl, combine seasoning sauce.

Heat a wok or large skillet over high heat until hot; add 3 tablespoons of oil and heat until hot. Stir-fry the ginger for about 5 seconds, scatter in the pork, and stir-fry briskly until it turns white. Add wood ears, tiger lily stems, dried shrimp, cabbage, bamboo shoots, and green onion. Cook for a few minutes, stirring constantly. Remove from wok.

Heat a wok or large skillet over high heat until hot; add 2 tablespoons of oil and heat until hot. Pour in the beaten eggs and stir-fry quickly until eggs are in small pieces. Return pork and other ingredients to the wok. Add seasoning sauce and mix well. Serve with Mandarin pancakes brushed with hoisin sauce if desired.

Serves 3 to 4.

PEARL BALLS
珍珠肉丸

When I was growing up in China many decades ago, it was a special treat to enjoy this dish, which required elaborate preparation. There were no grinders or food processors in those days, so my mother had to use Chinese cleavers to mince the pork. This took a lot of effort. Glutinous rice, after being cooked, becomes transparent. The meatballs, wrapped in rice, give the appearance of pearls; hence the dish's name. Nowadays, ground pork can be bought at any supermarket. If you don't eat pork, you can substitute chicken or beef.

INGREDIENTS
1 pound ground pork
1 cup glutinous rice (sweet rice)
8 water chestnuts, chopped
2 tablespoons Sichuan preserved mustard stems, minced
4 small dried Chinese mushrooms, minced
1 tablespoon dried shrimp, minced
2 tablespoons cornstarch
1 egg, well beaten
1 teaspoon sugar
1 tablespoon soy sauce
1 teaspoon salt
2 teaspoons sesame oil
2 teaspoons ginger, minced
2 tablespoons rice wine
½ teaspoon red pepper powder
Shredded carrot and chopped Chinese parsley (optional)

Wash rice well and soak in 2 cups of water for at least 2 hours. Drain well. Chop water chestnuts and mince Sichuan preserved mustard stems. Soak mushrooms and dried shrimp in hot water for 20 minutes. Discard the water and squeeze the mushrooms dry. Cut off and discard mushroom stems. Mince mushroom caps and softened dried shrimp.

Place all ingredients (except rice, water chestnuts, shredded carrot, and Chinese parsley) in a large bowl. Mix well with a fork, chopsticks, or electric mixer. Add water chestnuts. With wet hands, scoop up about 1 to 2 tablespoons of meat mixture and shape into a small, symmetrical ball. Repeat with remainder of mixture.

Roll each ball in rice to coat completely. Arrange meatballs in a steamer lined with a damp cloth or parchment paper and steam for about 25 minutes until rice is cooked. If desired, garnish pearl balls with shredded carrot and Chinese parsley before serving.

Makes about 24 large or 48 small pearl balls.

SHREDDED PORK WITH BROWN SAUCE
京醬肉絲

This is a simple dish to prepare, yet it tastes wonderful. You can serve it with plain boiled rice instead of pancakes. If you can't find hoisin sauce, you can use sweet bean sauce.

INGREDIENTS
1 pound pork tenderloin or pork loin
2 cups green onion, shredded
4 tablespoons oil
10 Mandarin pancakes (see page 136)

MARINADE
2 tablespoons soy sauce
2 teaspoons cornstarch
2 tablespoons rice wine

SEASONING SAUCE
4 tablespoons hoisin sauce
1 tablespoon sugar
2 tablespoons water

In a bowl, mix marinade. Cut the pork with the grain into ⅛-inch-thick slices, then cut against the grain into 2-inch-long shreds and marinate for 20 to 30 minutes. Shred the green onions. In a small bowl, combine seasoning sauce.

Heat a wok or large skillet over high heat until hot; add oil and heat until hot. Scatter in the pork and stir-fry briskly until it turns white. Add green onions and cook for another 20 seconds. Add seasoning sauce and stir thoroughly. Serve with Mandarin pancakes.

Serves 3 to 4.

SHREDDED PORK WITH HOT BEAN SAUCE
魚香肉絲

This dish actually is called "fish fragrant pork." Originally, someone was very clever to use the same kind of sauce made for fish to cook this pork dish. You can substitute beef, chicken, or turkey for pork. This dish goes very well with boiled rice. However, in my cooking classes and at home I often serve it with Mandarin pancakes. The pancakes are eaten like tacos.

INGREDIENTS
1 pound boneless pork
$\frac{1}{3}$ cup dried wood ears, shredded
1 cup bamboo shoots, shredded
1 tablespoon ginger, minced
1 tablespoon garlic, minced
4 tablespoons oil
1 whole green onion, chopped

MARINADE
1 tablespoon soy sauce
2 teaspoons cornstarch
1 tablespoon rice wine

SEASONING SAUCE
1 tablespoon hot bean sauce
2 tablespoons soy sauce
2 tablespoons rice wine
1 tablespoon vinegar
2 teaspoons sugar
2 teaspoons sesame oil
$\frac{1}{2}$ teaspoon salt
2 teaspoons cornstarch and 2 teaspoons
    water to make a paste

In a bowl, mix marinade. Cut the pork with the grain into $\frac{1}{8}$-inch-thick slices, then cut against the grain into 2-inch-long shreds and marinate for 20 to 30 minutes. Soak wood ears in hot water for 20 minutes. Shred wood ears and bamboo shoots. Mince ginger and garlic. In a small bowl, combine seasoning sauce.

Heat work or large skillet over high heat until hot; add oil and heat until hot. Stir-fry the ginger and garlic in oil for about 20 seconds, then scatter in the pork and stir-fry briskly until it turns white. Add wood ears and bamboo shoots and stir-fry for another 45 seconds. Add seasoning sauce and stir thoroughly. Sprinkle green onion over top and serve at once.

Serves 4 to 5.

SLICED PORK WITH GARLIC SAUCE
蒜泥肉片

When I prepare Double-Cooked Pork, I always cook double the amount of pork required. I use the other pound for Sliced Pork with Garlic Sauce. This dish usually is served at room temperature, but you can also serve it hot by reheating in the microwave. I use roasted garlic instead of raw mashed garlic. Because this dish can be prepared ahead of time, you might wish to serve it as one of the courses when you entertain. There is a very similar northern pork dish which simply adds 1 tablespoon of rice vinegar to the sauce.

INGREDIENTS
1 pound boneless pork in 1 piece
   (preferably center-cut boneless pork)
1 tablespoon rice wine
1 slice of ginger, smashed
1 whole green onion, smashed
Chinese parsley, chopped

SEASONING SAUCE
¼ cup soy sauce
¼ cup chicken stock
1 head roasted garlic, mashed*
½ teaspoon salt
1 tablespoon chili oil
2 tablespoons sesame oil
2 teaspoons sugar

Cut the pork into 9-inch x 1½-inch strips. Put the pork in a pot with enough water to cover. Bring to a boil with rice wine, ginger, and onion. Turn heat to medium-low to maintain a strong simmer; cover and cook for 25 minutes. Remove pork from water and let cool. After pork has cooled, cut the pork against the grain into ⅛-inch-thick slices. In a small bowl, combine seasoning sauce. Arrange the sliced pork in overlapping lines on a platter, then pour the sauce on top. Garnish with Chinese parsley.

Serves 3 to 4.

*Preheat oven to 350 degrees. Place the garlic on a large piece of foil, drizzle 1 tablespoon of oil on top, and wrap in foil. Place in the oven and roast for 50 minutes or until tender. Remove from the oven and let cool. Squeeze the garlic cloves from the head and place in a small bowl. With a fork, mash the garlic until smooth.

SPARERIBS WITH SEASONED RICE POWDER
粉蒸排骨

I grew up in Guizhou. Since Sichuan is a neighboring province, I learned to eat spicy food at a very young age. This spareribs recipe is a Sichuan dish of which I am very fond. We Chinese just love to eat pork and pork ribs. I remember when I taught Chinese cooking in the late 1970s, I had to make my own seasoned rice powder. Now I can buy it in any Chinese market.

INGREDIENTS
1½ pounds spareribs
2 packages (1.76 ounces each) seasoned
   rice powder

MARINADE
¼ teaspoon toasted Sichuan peppercorn
   powder (see page 169)
¼ teaspoon red pepper powder
½ teaspoon salt
1 teaspoon sugar
2 tablespoons soy sauce
2 tablespoons rice wine
1 teaspoon ginger, minced
1 teaspoon garlic, minced

Ask the butcher to chop the spareribs across the bones into 1¼-inch-long sections. Cut the spareribs between each rib, trimming off excess fat, until all the ribs are separated. Wash and pat dry with paper towels. In a bowl, mix marinade. Marinate the ribs for 20 to 30 minutes, stirring occasionally.

Pour the seasoned rice powder over the ribs evenly. Arrange the coated ribs in a heatproof dish or bowl. Now the ribs are ready to be steamed.

Place the dish or bowl of ribs in a steamer and steam over medium-high heat for 1½ hours. Make sure there is enough water in the steamer. If you have a small steamer, I suggest you have a pot of boiling water nearby to replenish the water in the steamer as needed.

Serves 3 to 4.

STEAMED SPARERIBS WITH FERMENTED BLACK BEANS
豆豉蒸排骨

This is a simple and delicious steamed dish. It can be prepared ahead of time and steamed 1½ hours before dinner is served. You can also pre-steam the dish and reheat it in the microwave. The fermented black beans give a distinctive flavor to this robust dish.

INGREDIENTS
1½ pounds spareribs
3 tablespoons fermented black beans, chopped
1 tablespoon ginger, minced
1 tablespoon garlic, minced
1 whole green onion, minced
1 small red chili pepper, chopped
1 whole green onion, chopped
1 to 2 tablespoons oil

SEASONING SAUCE
5 tablespoons soy sauce
2 tablespoons rice wine
1 tablespoon sugar

Ask the butcher to chop the spareribs across the bones into 1¼-inch-long sections. Cut the spareribs between each rib, trimming off excess fat, until all the ribs are separated. Wash and pat dry with paper towels. Set aside. Chop fermented black beans coarsely. Mince ginger, garlic, and green onion. Chop red chili pepper and green onion. In a small bowl, combine seasoning sauce.

Heat a wok or large skillet over high heat until hot; add oil and heat until hot. Stir-fry the fermented black beans, ginger, garlic, and green onion for 15 seconds. Add the spareribs and stir-fry briskly for 2 to 3 minutes until they become a little firm. Add the seasoning sauce and cook for about 1 minute. Remove from the wok and transfer to a heatproof dish or bowl. Now the ribs are ready to be steamed.

Place the dish or bowl of ribs in a steamer and steam over medium-high heat for 1½ hours. Garnish with chopped pepper and green onion before serving.

Serves 3 to 4.

STUFFED SPARERIBS WITH BROWN SAUCE
葱串排骨

The Chinese are very fond of spareribs, no matter how they're prepared. Most Asian supermarkets in the United States carry spareribs already pre-cut for you. When you prepare this dish, after the ribs have been cooked and the bones removed, you may find that the meat will rip apart as you insert the onion. I just use a toothpick to fasten the onion and the sparerib meat.

INGREDIENTS

2 pounds pork spareribs
30 whole green onions
2 whole star anises
¼ teaspoon Sichuan peppercorns
¼ teaspoon whole cloves
1 to 2 dried red peppers
4 slices ginger, smashed

4 cloves garlic, smashed
½ cup sugar
½ cup soy sauce
¼ cup rice wine
2 tablespoons rice vinegar
2 teaspoons sesame oil
Broccoli or lettuce (optional)

Cut the white part of 28 green onions into 2- to 3-inch-long pieces and remove the root ends. Smash the other 2 whole onions. Set aside.

Ask the butcher to chop the spareribs across the bones into 1¼-inch-long sections. Cut the spareribs between each rib, trimming off excess fat, until all the ribs are separated. Wash the ribs and place in a big pot covered with water. Bring water to a boil, then boil ribs for 5 minutes. Drain and wash the ribs again well.

Bring 3 cups of water to a boil in the same pot. Add smashed onion, star anises, peppercorns, cloves, dried red peppers, ginger, garlic, sugar, soy sauce, rice wine, and par-boiled ribs. Bring the mixture to a boil and simmer for 40 minutes with a cover. Remove the ribs from the pot and let cool. Turn the heat to high and cook the sauce until it is reduced to 1 cup. Add the vinegar to the reduced sauce and cook for another minute. Add the sesame oil. Keep the sauce warm in the oven (about 200 degrees).

Remove the bone from each of the ribs and insert one piece of cut onion into the hole. Stuff with onions until all the ribs are done. Put all of the stuffed spareribs in a heatproof dish, place in a steamer, and steam for 10 minutes. Pour the sauce over the steamed spareribs (drain the liquid from the heatproof dish if water is retained). If desired, garnish with blanched broccoli or lettuce bed on either side of the platter.

Serves 3 to 4.

SWEET AND SOUR PORK
甜酸肉

This is a very popular Cantonese dish. My brother David and his family have lived in San Francisco for more than 35 years. Many years ago, David and Carol (my sister-in-law) owned a restaurant there, and this dish was one of their customers' favorites. You can substitute chicken or beef for pork.

INGREDIENTS
1 pound lean pork
1 medium green pepper
3 slices fresh or canned pineapple
1 small onion
4 cups oil for deep-frying
1 teaspoon garlic, minced

MARINADE
1 tablespoon soy sauce
1 tablespoon rice wine
Dash white pepper

SEASONING SAUCE
7 tablespoons sugar
5 tablespoons rice vinegar
2 tablespoons ketchup
½ cup water
1½ tablespoons cornstarch

BATTER
½ cup flour
½ cup cornstarch
⅓ cup water or less to make a soft batter
½ teaspoon baking powder
1 egg, well beaten
½ teaspoon salt

In a bowl, mix marinade. Cut pork lengthwise into strips about 1 inch wide, then cut the strips crosswise into 1-inch cubes. Marinate for 20 to 30 minutes. Cut green pepper, remove seeds and membranes, and cut into 1-inch pieces. Next, cut pineapple and onion into pieces the same size as green pepper. Set aside. In a small bowl, combine seasoning sauce.

Heat a wok or large skillet over high heat until hot; add oil and heat to about 375 degrees. While oil is heating, mix batter in a bowl and coat the pork cubes thoroughly with batter. When oil is ready, drop pork cubes into the hot oil and deep-fry about 3 minutes, stirring constantly. Scoop out the meat with a skimmer. Increase the oil's temperature to 400 degrees; deep-fry the pork cubes once more until crispy and brown. Remove and drain.

Heat a wok or large skillet over high heat until hot; add 2 tablespoons of oil and heat until hot. Stir-fry the garlic, pineapple, green pepper, and onion for about 2 minutes. Add seasoning sauce and stir until it thickens. Add the pork, mix well, and serve.

Serves 3 to 4.

Beef

ANTS CLIMBING A TREE
螞蟻上樹

Cellophane noodles are also called bean thread or transparent vermicelli. This dish is cooked with ground beef. Once the beef and the cellophane noodles are cooked in a brown sauce, the noodles resemble tree bark and the ground beef looks like ants. This Sichuan dish is quite popular among the Chinese.

INGREDIENTS
3 packages (1.3 ounces each) cellophane
  noodles
¼ pound ground beef
2 tablespoons green onion, chopped
1 teaspoon ginger, minced
2 tablespoons oil
1 tablespoon hot bean sauce

SEASONING SAUCE
1 cup chicken stock
1 tablespoon soy sauce
1 tablespoon rice wine
1 teaspoon sugar

Soak cellophane noodles in hot water until soft (about 10 to 12 minutes), then cut with scissors into shorter pieces, 6 to 8 inches in length. Rinse and drain. Chop green onion and mince ginger. In a small bowl, combine seasoning sauce.

Heat a wok or large skillet over high heat until hot; add oil and heat until hot. Stir-fry the beef until it separates into bits; add green onion, ginger, and hot bean sauce. Stir and mix well. Add the cellophane noodles and the seasoning sauce, stirring occasionally. Turn heat to medium-high; cook until the liquid almost evaporates.

Serves 3 to 4.

BEEF STEAK ON SIZZLING PLATE
鐵板牛排

If you like to eat steak, this dish is for you. I highly recommend that you use flank steak instead of more expensive cuts of beef. Using a large, non-stick frying pan to pan-fry the beef will make the job a lot easier. Since there is no green vegetable in this dish, you actually can cook it a day in advance and reheat it in the microwave before serving. You will really impress your family and friends when you serve it on a sizzling cast iron plate.

INGREDIENTS
1 pound flank steak
¼ cup cornstarch
1 large onion, sliced
½ to 1 small Jamaica red pepper, sliced
8 tablespoons oil

SEASONING SAUCE
3 tablespoons tomato ketchup
3 tablespoons water
1 tablespoon rice wine
1 tablespoon oyster sauce
2 teaspoons rice vinegar
2 teaspoons sugar

MARINADE
1 tablespoon soy sauce
1 tablespoon rice wine
1 whole green onion, smashed
4 slices ginger, smashed

Lay beef flat and hold the cleaver at a slant nearly parallel to the cutting board; slice the beef into ¼-inch x 2½-inch x 5-inch pieces. Place in a bowl, add the marinade ingredients, and toss lightly to coat. Marinate for at least 30 minutes (or refrigerate for up to 4 hours). Remove beef pieces from the marinade and carefully dredge them in cornstarch. Slice the onion and Jamaica red pepper and discard the seeds. Preheat the cast iron plate in a 350-degree oven. In a small bowl, combine seasoning sauce.

Heat a wok or large skillet over high heat until hot; add 6 tablespoons of oil and heat until hot. Pan-fry the marinated beef until brown on both sides (about 1 minute each side). Keep the beef warm on a plate. Heat a wok or large skillet over high heat until hot; add 2 tablespoons of oil and heat until hot. Add sliced onion and red pepper and stir-fry for about 2 minutes. Add the warm beef. Add the seasoning sauce until the mixture is evenly coated. Serve on the hot cast iron plate.

Serves 3 to 4.

BEEF WITH BROCCOLI
芥藍牛肉

Broccoli is available year-round and is one of the best green vegetables you can eat. It is an excellent source of vitamins A and C, as well as calcium and iron. This is one of my son Christopher's favorite dishes. You can substitute chicken or pork for beef.

INGREDIENTS
1 pound flank steak
3 to 4 cups broccoli
1 whole green onion, minced
1 teaspoon ginger, minced
4 tablespoons oil

SEASONING SAUCE
2 tablespoons soy sauce
2 tablespoons oyster sauce
2 teaspoons cornstarch and 2 teaspoons water to make a paste
2 teaspoons sugar

MARINADE
1 tablespoon soy sauce
1 tablespoon rice wine
½ tablespoon cornstarch
½ teaspoon sugar

In a bowl, mix marinade. Cut meat with the grain into 2-inch-wide strips. Then cut crosswise against the grain into ⅛-inch slices and marinate for 20 to 30 minutes. Cut off the broccoli florets. Peel off the tough outer skin of the stems with a sharp knife. Slice the stems diagonally into 2-inch pieces. Mince green onion and ginger. In a small bowl, combine seasoning sauce.

Heat a wok or large skillet over high heat until hot; add oil and heat until hot. Stir-fry the ginger and green onion for about 5 seconds, add the beef and stir-fry briskly for 2 to 3 minutes until it becomes firm. Bring a large pot of water to a boil and cook the broccoli for about 20 seconds. Drain into a colander. Add broccoli to the meat, toss the mixture, then add seasoning sauce. Stir until beef and broccoli are evenly coated with seasoning sauce.

Serves 3 to 4.

BEEF WITH GREEN PEPPERS
青椒牛肉

In the United States, you can purchase green peppers just about all year round. In fact, this dish can also be made from a variety of peppers, such as red peppers, orange peppers, and yellow peppers. During the Christmas season, I like to cook this dish with green peppers and red peppers. Since these kinds of peppers can be eaten raw, I don't cook them very long.

INGREDIENTS
1 pound flank steak
2 to 3 cups green peppers, shredded
1 whole green onion, minced
1 teaspoon ginger, minced
4 tablespoons oil

SEASONING SAUCE
2 tablespoons soy sauce
2 tablespoons oyster sauce
2 tablespoons rice wine
2 teaspoons cornstarch and 2 teaspoons
   water to make a paste
2 teaspoons sugar

MARINADE
1 tablespoon soy sauce
1 tablespoon rice wine
½ tablespoon cornstarch
½ teaspoon sugar

In a bowl, mix marinade. Cut the beef against the grain into ⅛-inch-thick slices, then cut again into 2-inch-long shreds and marinate for 20 to 30 minutes. Shred the peppers and put them aside. Mince green onion and ginger. In a small bowl, combine seasoning sauce.

Heat a wok or large skillet over high heat until hot; add oil and heat until hot. Stir-fry the ginger and green onion for about 5 seconds; add the beef and stir-fry briskly for 2 to 3 minutes until it becomes firm. Add shredded peppers to beef and cook for another minute, then add seasoning sauce. Stir until beef and green peppers are evenly coated with seasoning sauce.

Serves 3 to 4.

BEEF WITH SNOW PEAS
雪豆牛肉

Snow peas are a must in Chinese cooking. To transform snow peas from ordinary green to jade green in color, you can either deep-fry them in oil or parboil them in boiling water. Since nowadays everybody is worried about calorie intake, I always use the parboil method. The result is very satisfying.

INGREDIENTS
1 pound flank steak
2 to 3 cups snow peas
1 whole green onion, minced
1 teaspoon ginger, minced
4 tablespoons oil

SEASONING SAUCE
2 tablespoons soy sauce
2 tablespoons oyster sauce
2 tablespoons rice wine
2 teaspoons cornstarch and 2 teaspoons
   water to make a paste
2 teaspoons sugar

MARINADE
1 tablespoon soy sauce
1 tablespoon rice wine
½ tablespoon cornstarch
½ teaspoon sugar

In a bowl, mix marinade. Cut meat with the grain into 2-inch-wide strips. Then cut crosswise against the grain into ⅛-inch slices and marinate for 20 to 30 minutes. String the snow peas and set aside. Mince green onion and ginger. In a small bowl, combine seasoning sauce.

Heat a wok or large skillet over high heat until hot; add oil and heat until hot. Stir-fry the ginger and green onion for about 5 seconds. Add the beef and stir-fry briskly for 2 to 3 minutes until it becomes firm. Bring a large pot of water to a boil and cook the snow peas for about 15 seconds. Drain into a colander. Add snow peas to the meat, toss the mixture, then add seasoning sauce. Stir until beef and snow peas are evenly coated with seasoning sauce.

Serves 3 to 4.

CRISPY BEEF
脆皮牛肉

My students often ask me to recommend reputable Chinese restaurants in our area. My answer is that my husband and I seldom eat out. But when we do I almost always order crispy beef as my first choice. Since I am not that fond of deep-frying, I enjoy letting someone else cook deep-fried dishes for me. If you prefer extra crispiness, you can deep-fry this dish a second time in hot oil (about 400 degrees) for 1 to 2 minutes.

INGREDIENTS
1 pound lean beef (flank steak or beef tenderloin)
1 cup cornstarch
At least 2 cups oil for deep-frying
1 tablespoon roasted sesame seeds
3 tablespoons green onion, minced

SEASONING SAUCE
3 tablespoons soy sauce
4 tablespoons rice vinegar
6 tablespoons sugar
1 to 2 teaspoons chili oil
2 tablespoons cornstarch and 2 tablespoons water to make a paste

Cut the beef with the grain into 2-inch-wide strips. Then cut crosswise against the grain into ⅛-inch slices. Coat beef with cornstarch thoroughly and set aside. In a small bowl, combine seasoning sauce.

Heat oil in a wok or large skillet until hot (about 375 degrees). Deep-fry the beef slices until golden brown. Remove and drain. Keep warm. Heat the seasoning sauce in a small pot over medium-high heat until the sauce is thick and clear. Pour sauce over the beef. Remove the crispy beef to a warm platter and sprinkle roasted sesame seeds and minced green onion on top.

Serves 2 to 3.

ORANGE BEEF
橘子牛肉

This is another favorite deep-fried dish among Americans and Chinese people. Most recipes call for using dried tangerine peels, but I discovered that fresh orange peels and orange juice make the sauce just as tasty. I reduce the amount of fat by using stir-frying instead of deep-frying to cook this dish. If you prefer your dishes spicy, simply increase the number of red peppers.

INGREDIENTS
1 pound flank steak
Zest from 1 medium-sized orange, minced
5 to 6 dried red peppers
2 teaspoons ginger, minced
2 teaspoons garlic, minced
3 to 4 tablespoons oil
2 whole green onions, chopped

SEASONING SAUCE
3 tablespoons dark soy sauce
2 tablespoons sugar
1 teaspoon sesame oil
1 teaspoon rice vinegar
1 tablespoon rice wine
¼ cup fresh orange juice
2 teaspoons cornstarch and 2 teaspoons
    water to make a paste

MARINADE
1 tablespoon dark soy sauce
1 tablespoon rice wine
1 tablespoon water
2 teaspoons cornstarch

In a bowl, mix marinade. Cut meat with the grain into 2-inch-wide strips. Then cut crosswise against the grain into ⅛-inch slices and marinate for 20 to 30 minutes. In a small bowl, combine seasoning sauce.

Heat a wok or large skillet over high heat until hot; add oil and heat until hot. Toss in zest and dried red peppers, pressing them into the oil until they turn dark. Add minced ginger and garlic and stir-fry for about 30 seconds. Add the beef and stir-fry for about 2 minutes until the pieces are firm, then add the seasoning sauce and stir until mixture thickens. Remove to a serving dish and garnish with green onions.

Serves 2 to 3.

RICE POWDER STEAMED BEEF
粉蒸牛肉

I remember when I was a youngster my mother loved to occasionally prepare this favorite dish for the family as our Sunday meal. Pork was more accessible, so we ate steamed pork more often than steamed beef. If you are fond of this dish, why not make a double recipe, eating one and freezing the other? You will discover that the flavor is enhanced the next day. You can substitute parsnip for sweet potato, if you wish.

INGREDIENTS
½ pound flank steak
3 packages (1.76 ounces each) seasoned
   rice powder or ½ cup homemade rice
   powder (see below)
1 small sweet potato, sliced

HOMEMADE RICE POWDER
1 cup long-grain rice
½ teaspoon each of cumin, anise seed,
   cinnamon, and white pepper
1 teaspoon Sichuan peppercorns

MARINADE
1 whole green onion, minced
1 teaspoon ginger, minced
1 tablespoon soy sauce
1 tablespoon hot bean sauce
1 teaspoon sweet bean sauce
1 teaspoon rice wine
1 teaspoon sugar
½ to 1 teaspoon red pepper powder
2 tablespoons oil

In a bowl, mix marinade. Cut meat with the grain into 2-inch-wide strips. Then cut crosswise against the grain into ⅛-inch slices and marinate for 20 to 30 minutes.

To make your homemade rice powder: Stir-fry the rice mixture without oil over medium-low heat for 5 minutes, then for 5 more minutes over low heat. After the rice mixture cools off, grind in a blender or food processor until fine.

Dredge each piece of meat thoroughly with rice powder. Place meat on a greased pie pan or heatproof dish and put slices of sweet potato on top. Steam for 20 minutes. Before serving, invert pie pan or heatproof dish on a serving dish so that meat is on top of potatoes.

Serves 2 to 3.

SESAME BEEF
芝麻牛肉

You can select any vegetable you can find in the supermarket or Asian market – such as spinach, broccoli, or asparagus – to substitute for watercress. You may want to blanch the asparagus for 1 to 2 minutes.

In China, a typical stir-fried dish consists of a little meat and a lot of vegetables. I usually cook 1 pound of meat or poultry and add 2 to 4 cups of vegetables. This dish can't be cooked ahead of time and reheated. It has to be cooked just before serving.

INGREDIENTS
1 pound flank steak
2 teaspoons salt
1 pound watercress
2 tablespoons green onion, chopped
1 teaspoon ginger, minced
1 teaspoon garlic, minced
5 tablespoons oil
1 tablespoon roasted sesame seeds

SEASONING SAUCE
2 tablespoons raw sesame seeds
3 tablespoons soy sauce
2 tablespoons rice wine
1 tablespoon water
1½ tablespoons sesame oil
2 teaspoons sugar
¼ teaspoon freshly ground black pepper

MARINADE
1 tablespoon soy sauce
1 tablespoon water
1 tablespoon rice wine
2 teaspoons cornstarch

In a bowl, mix marinade. Cut meat with the grain into 2-inch-wide strips. Then cut crosswise against the grain into ⅛-inch slices and marinate for 20 to 30 minutes. Boil 8 cups water with 2 teaspoons salt in a deep pot. Add watercress and blanch 15 seconds. Drain well. Transfer to a serving platter. Chop green onion and mince ginger and garlic. In a small bowl, combine seasoning sauce.

Heat a wok or large skillet over high heat until hot; add 4 tablespoons of oil and heat until hot. Stir-fry the beef until it becomes firm (about 2 to 3 minutes). Set aside. Stir-fry green onion, ginger, and garlic in 1 tablespoon of oil until fragrant. Add seasoning sauce and bring to a boil. Stir in beef and cook over high heat until sauce is half evaporated. Spoon beef and sauce over watercress and sprinkle with roasted sesame seeds.

Serves 3 to 4.

SPICY BEEF WITH CELERY AND CARROTS
乾煸牛肉絲

This is a typical Sichuan dish, hot and tasty, that should please lovers of spicy food. Many Chinese people enjoy it even more when it is served at room temperature. Beef is eaten much less frequently in China than pork. In southern China, beef is usually water buffalo or ox, so the meat is often tough and chewy.

INGREDIENTS
1 pound flank steak
2 cups celery, shredded
1 cup carrots, shredded
3 fresh or dried red peppers
1 whole green onion, chopped
1 teaspoon ginger, minced
5 tablespoons oil
1 tablespoon hot bean sauce

SEASONING
1 teaspoon sesame oil
¼ teaspoon toasted Sichuan peppercorn
   powder (see page 169)
1 teaspoon rice vinegar

MARINADE
3 tablespoons soy sauce
1 tablespoon rice wine
1 teaspoon sugar

In a bowl, mix marinade. Cut the beef against the grain into ⅛-inch-thick slices, then cut again into 2-inch-long strips and marinate for 20 to 30 minutes. Remove the leaves and wash the celery, then dry and shred it. Peel and shred the carrots. Top and seed the fresh red peppers and cut them lengthwise into fine shreds. If using dried red peppers, top and seed them and cut them lengthwise into fine shreds with scissors. Chop green onion and mince ginger. Put seasoning ingredients in a small container.

Heat a wok or large skillet over high heat until hot; add 2 tablespoons of oil and heat until hot. Stir-fry celery, carrots, and red pepper, then toss them over high heat until they are almost cooked. Remove and drain. Heat the same wok or skillet. Add 3 tablespoons of oil and stir-fry the beef over high heat until the meat is dry and no liquid is left. The beef should be dry-looking and stiff. When the beef is cooked, add hot bean sauce, ginger, and green onion, and cook for a few seconds. Add vegetables and seasoning and stir thoroughly.

Serves 3 to 4.

Chicken and Duck

BON BON CHICKEN
棒棒雞

I grew up in Guizhou before my family moved to Taiwan. Since Guizhou is a province neighboring Sichuan, I learned to eat fiery hot food at a very young age. Bon Bon Chicken is one of the favorite spicy dishes in our family. This is a dish that you can prepare ahead of time. It is great as an appetizer or as a regular course.

INGREDIENTS

1 pound chicken breasts with bones
1 tablespoon rice wine
1 slice ginger, smashed
1 whole green onion, smashed
1 large cucumber, shredded
¼ teaspoon salt
1 piece mung bean sheet, shredded
1 tablespoon green onion, minced
2 teaspoons ginger, minced
2 teaspoons garlic, minced
¼ teaspoon toasted Sichuan peppercorn
   powder (see page 169)

SEASONING SAUCE

2 tablespoons sesame seed paste
3 tablespoons soy sauce
1 tablespoon rice vinegar
1 tablespoon sesame oil
1 teaspoon chili oil
2 teaspoons sugar

Place chicken breasts in a deep pot of cold water and cook over high heat until water boils. Add rice wine, ginger, and green onion. Turn heat to medium-low and cook 15 to 20 minutes. Remove and drain. After the chicken cools off, remove the bones and shred the chicken into thin strips.

Shred cucumber, sprinkle with salt, and let stand about 10 minutes. Squeeze water out of cucumber and set aside. Soak mung bean sheet in boiling water for about 30 minutes, then shred. Mince green onion, ginger, and garlic. In a small bowl, combine seasoning sauce.

Spread shredded cucumbers on a round serving plate. Place shredded mung bean sheet on top of cucumber. Place shredded chicken on top of shredded mung bean sheet. Sprinkle with green onion, ginger, garlic, and toasted Sichuan peppercorn powder. Pour seasoning sauce over the chicken and mix carefully before serving.

Serves 2 to 3.

CHICKEN CHENDU STYLE
成都子雞

Chendu is the capital of Sichuan Province. You can use boneless chicken to prepare this dish, but it definitely tastes superior when cooked with the bone. It goes well with plain boiled rice.

INGREDIENTS
1½ pounds chicken with bones (breasts or thighs)
½ cup celery, chopped
½ cup green onion, chopped
2 tablespoons oil
2 teaspoons cornstarch and 2 teaspoons water to make a paste

SEASONING SAUCE
2 small pickled hot peppers, chopped
2 tablespoons hot bean sauce
½ teaspoon toasted Sichuan peppercorn powder (see page 169)
1 tablespoon rice wine
1 teaspoon sugar
½ teaspoon salt
1 tablespoon vinegar
½ tablespoon ginger, minced
½ tablespoon garlic, minced

Wash and pat the chicken dry with paper towels. With a meat cleaver or sharp knife, cut chicken through the bone into 2-inch pieces. Chop celery, green onion, and pickled hot pepper. Mince ginger and garlic. In a small bowl, combine seasoning sauce.

Heat a wok or large skillet over high heat until hot; add oil and heat until hot. Add the chicken and stir-fry until the pieces are white and firm (about 2 minutes). Add seasoning sauce and ½ cup water; cook for 2 to 3 minutes. After mixture comes to a boil, cover and simmer for 10 to 15 minutes. Remove cover and stir in cornstarch paste until mixture thickens. Sprinkle with celery and green onions. Mix well and serve.

Serves 2 to 3.

Chicken Salad With Mung Bean Sheets
涼拌雞絲

Over the years I have tried to introduce mung bean sheets to my students. If you have a hard time finding this product, you can substitute cellophane noodles (bean thread noodles). Where I am living now, many Korean-owned grocery stores don't carry mung bean sheets, so I usually have to make a special trip to a Chinese grocery store. This salad can be served year round, but it's best eaten in the hot summer.

INGREDIENTS

3 pounds chicken breasts with bones
1 tablespoon rice wine
1 slice ginger, smashed
1 whole green onion, smashed
2 mung bean sheets
1 cup carrot, shredded
2 cups cucumber, shredded
Roasted sesame seeds or crushed roasted
  peanuts
Chinese parsley, chopped

SEASONING SAUCE

¼ cup soy sauce
2 tablespoons sesame paste
½ cup fresh lime juice
6 tablespoons sesame oil
1 to 2 teaspoons chili oil
2 teaspoons sugar
½ teaspoon salt
1 tablespoon garlic, minced
2 teaspoons ginger, minced

Place chicken breasts in a deep pot of cold water and cook over high heat until water boils. Add rice wine, ginger, and green onion. Turn heat to medium-low and cook 15 to 20 minutes. Remove and drain. After the chicken cools off, remove the bones and shred the chicken into thin strips. In a large bowl, pour boiling water over the mung bean sheets and let them soak for 30 minutes. Shred carrot and cucumber. In a small bowl, combine seasoning sauce.

Drain the mung bean sheets. Remove them to the cutting board and cut them into shreds. Place the shredded mung bean sheets on a serving platter. Spread the shredded carrots and cucumbers on top, leaving a ½-inch border of shredded mung bean sheets. Scatter the chicken shreds over the carrots and cucumbers, leaving a narrow border of carrot and cucumber mixture.

Just before serving, pour seasoning sauce over the chicken mixture and sprinkle with sesame seeds or crushed peanuts. Garnish with fresh Chinese parsley. Serve the salad at room temperature or chilled.

Serves 5 to 6.

CHICKEN WITH HOT AND SPICY SAUCE
麻辣白切雞

This Sichuan dish, pungent and spicy with fresh herbs, will certainly wake you up! If your friends and family don't want the dish to be too hot and spicy, you can simply reduce the amount of chili oil and Sichuan peppercorn powder. I usually serve this dish with boiled rice.

INGREDIENTS
1 whole chicken (about 3 to 3½ pounds)
    or 2 pounds chicken breasts with bones
1 teaspoon salt
Chinese parsley, chopped (optional)

SEASONING SAUCE
1 whole green onion, minced
2 teaspoons ginger, minced
2 teaspoons garlic, minced
3 tablespoons soy sauce
1 tablespoon rice vinegar
3 tablespoons sesame oil
½ to 1 teaspoon toasted Sichuan
    peppercorn powder (see page 169)
2 teaspoons sugar
1 to 2 teaspoons chili oil

Wash and clean the whole chicken thoroughly. Dry with paper towels. Put the chicken in a shallow heatproof bowl or container, rub the salt all over the chicken, and put in the refrigerator for 4 to 5 hours or overnight.

Use a large steamer and steam the chicken on high heat for one hour. (If you use chicken breasts with bones, reduce the steaming time to 30 minutes.) Make sure there is plenty of water in the steamer to keep the steam going strong. When the chicken is cooked, let it cool. While the chicken is being steamed, combine seasoning sauce in a small bowl.

Remove the bones from the chicken and cut into ½-inch pieces. Put the boneless chicken pieces into a heatproof bowl and steam another 5 minutes.

Before serving, invert the bowl on a serving dish so that the chicken pieces are attractively displayed, then pour the seasoning sauce over them. You can also serve this dish at room temperature. Garnish with Chinese parsley if desired.

Serves 3 to 4.

CHICKEN WITH PEANUTS
宮保雞丁

This famous dish is called Kung Pao Chicken in Mandarin. There is a true story behind this well-known dish. Mr. Ting Kung Pao received an appointment as an imperial official to Sichuan in the 1800s. Cooking was one of his hobbies. Mr. Ting prepared this dish for his friends, and it took his name. Be very careful when the red peppers are being charred. Please remember to open a window or turn your exhaust fan to high speed to avoid choking and coughing.

INGREDIENTS
1 pound boneless chicken meat
5 to 6 dried red peppers
4 tablespoons oil
1 teaspoon ginger, minced
½ cup roasted peanuts

SEASONING SAUCE
2 tablespoons dark soy sauce
2 tablespoons rice wine
2 teaspoons rice vinegar
4 teaspoons sugar
2 teaspoons sesame oil
2 tablespoons water
2 teaspoons cornstarch

MARINADE
½ egg white, beaten
1 tablespoon dark soy sauce
½ tablespoon cornstarch

In a bowl, mix marinade. Cut chicken with the grain into ½-inch-wide strips. Then cut crosswise against the grain into ½-inch dice and marinate for 20 to 30 minutes. Wipe clean and remove tips and seeds of dried red peppers. Use scissors to cut diagonally into ½-inch-long pieces or leave them whole. In a small bowl, combine seasoning sauce.

Heat a wok or large skillet over high heat until hot; add oil and heat until hot. Toss in dried red peppers, pressing them into the oil until they turn dark. Add minced ginger and stir-fry for about 30 seconds. Add the chicken and stir-fry until the pieces are white and firm (about 2 minutes), then add the seasoning sauce and stir until it thickens. Turn off the heat. Add the peanuts and mix well just before serving.

Serves 3 to 4.

CHICKEN WITH PINE NUTS
松子雞米

Pine nuts are used in cooking all over the world: in Italy for pesto sauce, in the Middle East for adding to meat, rice, and vegetable dishes, etc. This is a very easy dish to make. It is light, delicate, and flavorful.

INGREDIENTS
1 pound boneless and skinless chicken
   breasts
½ cup roasted pine nuts
2 cups celery, diced
1 teaspoon ginger, minced
4 tablespoons oil

SEASONING SAUCE
1 teaspoon chili oil
½ teaspoon salt
1 teaspoon cornstarch
3 tablespoons chicken stock
½ teaspoon white pepper

MARINADE
1 egg white, beaten
2 teaspoons cornstarch
1 tablespoon rice wine
½ teaspoon sugar
¼ teaspoon salt
2 teaspoons sesame oil

Preheat oven to 300 degrees. In a bowl, mix marinade. Cut chicken with the grain into ¼-inch strips. Put the strips together and cut across the grain into ¼-inch dice, then marinate for 20 to 30 minutes. Bake pine nuts until brown (about 8 to 10 minutes). Set them aside. Dice celery into ¼-inch pieces and mince ginger. In a small bowl, combine seasoning sauce.

Heat a wok or large skillet over high heat until hot; add 3 tablespoons of oil and heat until hot. Add the chicken and stir-fry until the pieces are white and firm (about 2 minutes). Remove chicken to a plate. Bring a large pot of water to a boil and cook the celery for about 20 seconds. Drain into a colander.

Return the wok or large skillet to high heat; add 1 tablespoon of oil and heat until hot. Stir-fry ginger for a few seconds. Add chicken, celery, and seasoning sauce. Stir until all the ingredients are coated with a light, clear glaze. Pour mixture onto a heated platter and serve at once with pine nuts sprinkled on top.

Serves 3 to 4.

CURRY CHICKEN WITH BROCCOLI
咖喱芥蘭雞

I created this dish several years ago. I thought it was a little odd that my mother always cooked this dish with potatoes, as is called for in other Chinese cookbooks I have read. I must admit that I am not that fond of that method. Since I love rice and broccoli, the rest is history. If you like a little color in this dish, you can add peeled, sliced carrots.

INGREDIENTS
1 pound boneless and skinless chicken
   breasts
4 cups broccoli
1 teaspoon garlic, minced
4 tablespoons oil

SEASONING SAUCE
1 tablespoon curry powder
1 teaspoon salt
1¾ cups chicken stock (see page 18)
   or water
¼ cup cornstarch and ¼ cup water to make
   a paste

MARINADE
1 tablespoon soy sauce
½ tablespoon cornstarch
1 tablespoon rice wine

In a bowl, mix marinade. Cut chicken with the grain into 2-inch-wide strips. Then cut crosswise against the grain into ⅛-inch slices and marinate for 20 to 30 minutes. Cut off the broccoli florets. With a sharp knife, peel off the tough outer skin of the broccoli stems. Slice the broccoli stems diagonally into 2-inch pieces. Mince garlic. In a small bowl, combine seasoning sauce.

Heat a wok or large skillet over high heat until hot; add oil and heat until hot. Add garlic and stir-fry for a few seconds. Add the chicken and stir-fry until the pieces are white and firm (about 2 minutes). Add seasoning sauce and cook until mixture boils. Add the broccoli and cook another 30 seconds. Stir until chicken and vegetables are coated with sauce. Serve on top of plain boiled rice.

Serves 3 to 4.

DICED CHICKEN WITH VEGETABLES
炒雞丁

When I teach this dish in my cooking class, I always double the recipe: one cooked with white meat, the other with dark meat. Most of my students like the version with dark meat better. This is such a simple dish, yet it is very tasty, using vegetables in season. If you prefer this dish a little spicy, add one or two minced fresh chili peppers to the ginger and garlic when you first stir-fry them. You can also add your favorite nuts to this dish, such as almonds, cashews, or walnuts.

INGREDIENTS
1 pound boneless chicken (breasts or thighs)
1 whole green onion, minced
1 teaspoon ginger, minced
1 teaspoon garlic, minced
3 to 4 cups of fresh vegetables, diced (broccoli, carrots, water chestnuts, green and red peppers)
4 tablespoons oil

SEASONING SAUCE
1 tablespoon rice wine
2 tablespoons soy sauce
1 tablespoon rice vinegar
½ teaspoon salt
1 teaspoon sugar
1 tablespoon sesame oil
2 teaspoons cornstarch
2 tablespoons water

MARINADE
1 tablespoon soy sauce
1 tablespoon rice wine
½ tablespoon cornstarch

In a bowl, mix marinade. Cut the chicken lengthwise into ½-inch strips, then cut the strips crosswise to make ½-inch squares and marinate for 20 to 30 minutes. Mince green onion, ginger, and garlic. Cut fresh vegetables the same size as the chicken. In a small bowl, combine seasoning sauce. Blanch the vegetables (but not the peppers) in boiling water for about 45 seconds, then pour them immediately into a colander.

Heat a wok or large skillet over high heat until hot; add 4 tablespoons of oil and heat until hot. Scatter in the minced onion, ginger, and garlic and stir-fry for 5 seconds. Add the chicken and stir-fry until the pieces are white and firm (about 2 minutes). Add green peppers or red peppers to the chicken pieces and stir-fry for another minute. Add blanched vegetables and seasoning sauce, stirring in a circular motion until the chicken and vegetables are smoothly glazed. Pour into a serving dish.

Serves 3 to 4.

EIGHT-JEWEL DUCK
八寶鴨

This classic dish is definitely a labor of love, and it does take a little effort to make it. The best part about making this dish is that the preparation can be done in advance. The original way to make this duck is steamed and then deep-fried until golden brown. I use the oven method, and the result is still spectacular: crisp skin, moist meat, and delicious stuffing.

INGREDIENTS

1 duck (about 4 to 5 pounds)
1 cup glutinous rice (sweet rice)
4 dried Chinese mushrooms, diced
1 tablespoon dried shrimp
2 tablespoons oil
½ cup country ham or Chinese sausage, diced
½ cup bamboo shoots, diced
1 small carrot, peeled and diced
¼ cup pine nuts
3 tablespoons fresh soy beans
1 tablespoon soy sauce
Chinese parsley, chopped (optional)
Toasted Sichuan peppercorn powder (see page 169) and salt

SEASONING SAUCE

1 tablespoon rice wine
2 tablespoons soy sauce
½ teaspoon salt
½ teaspoon sugar
¼ teaspoon white pepper

Wash rice well and soak in 2 cups of water for at least 2 hours. Drain well. Place the rice in a steamer lined with a damp cloth or parchment paper. Steam for 45 minutes. Turn off the heat and let rice stand for another 15 minutes.

Bone the duck and set it aside (see directions on page 13). Soak mushrooms and shrimp in hot water for 20 minutes. Discard the water and squeeze the mushrooms dry. Cut off and discard mushroom stems, then cut each cap into ¼-inch dice. Chop softened dried shrimp coarsely. In a small bowl, combine seasoning sauce.

Heat a wok or large skillet over high heat until hot; add oil and heat until hot. Stir-fry shrimp, ham or sausage, bamboo shoots, carrot, nuts, and soybeans for 2 minutes. Add seasoning sauce while stirring constantly. Turn off the heat. Add the glutinous rice and mix thoroughly with the other ingredients. This is the stuffing.

Use needle and thread to sew the neck opening of the duck. Pack the stuffing loosely into the cavity of the duck and close the tail opening with needle and thread. Place the stuffed boneless duck on its back in a steamer and steam for 1¼ hours over high heat. Remove from steamer.

Preheat oven to 400 degrees. Brush the duck with 1 tablespoon soy sauce. Grease a roasting rack, put duck on rack, turn oven down to 350 degrees, and roast the duck for 1 hour. When duck is done, remove the thread. Place the duck on a cutting board and cut lengthwise in half, then crosswise into 8 to 9 pieces as desired. Place the duck on a platter and garnish with Chinese parsley if desired. Serve with Sichuan peppercorn and salt.

Serves 4 to 5.

GENERAL TSO'S CHICKEN
左公雞

A dish named after a general certainly sounds impressive. For example, there is Beef Wellington, reminding us of the British general who defeated Napoleon. General Tso was a regional leader of Sichuan in the mid-1800s, but the dish named after him was definitely invented in America. The same is true of Chinese fortune cookies. You can deep-fry the chicken one day in advance and deep-fry it again just before you are ready to serve. Stir-fry with red peppers, ginger, garlic, and seasoning sauce during the last few minutes.

INGREDIENTS
1 pound boneless chicken (breasts or thighs)
1 tablespoon ginger, minced
1 tablespoon garlic, minced
3 cups oil for deep-frying
2 to 3 dried red peppers
2 whole green onions, chopped

SEASONING SAUCE
¼ cup dark soy sauce
½ cup sugar
1 tablespoon rice wine
1 tablespoon vinegar
1 tablespoon cornstarch
5 tablespoons water
2 teaspoons sesame oil

MARINADE
1 egg white, beaten
1 tablespoon rice wine
Pinch of freshly ground white pepper
2 tablespoons oil
¼ cup cornstarch

In a bowl, mix marinade. Clean chicken and pat dry. Cut chicken lengthwise into 1-inch-wide strips, then cut again crosswise into 1-inch pieces and marinate for 20 to 30 minutes. Mince ginger and garlic. In a small bowl, combine seasoning sauce.

Heat a wok over high heat for 1 minute. Add the oil and heat to 375 degrees. Place the chicken, one piece at a time, in the oil and cook for 2 minutes until slightly brown. Remove the chicken pieces from the oil and let them drain in a colander for 10 minutes. Heat the oil again to 425 degrees. Place the chicken again in the hot oil and cook to golden brown. Remove from the oil and drain.

Heat a wok or large skillet over high heat until hot; add 2 tablespoons of oil and heat until hot. Add the dried red peppers and cook until darkened. Add the ginger and garlic and stir briefly. Add the seasoning sauce and stir until it thickens. Add the chicken pieces and coat well. Remove to a serving dish and garnish with green onions.

Serves 3 to 4.

GENERAL TSO'S CHICKEN, STIR-FRIED
炒左公雞

General Tso's chicken is normally always deep-fried, whether it is prepared at the restaurant or at home. It is delicious, with crispy skin and succulent sauce, but it doesn't help your waistline if you are counting calories. I use this stir-frying technique to reduce the fat content, and the result is quite satisfying. The sauce is tasty and goes well with plain boiled rice.

INGREDIENTS
1 pound boneless chicken (breasts or thighs)
6 dried red peppers
2 teaspoons ginger, minced
2 teaspoons garlic, minced
4 tablespoons oil
12 ounces broccoli florets

SEASONING SAUCE
2 tablespoons dark soy sauce
¼ cup sugar
½ tablespoon rice wine
½ tablespoon rice vinegar
2 teaspoons cornstarch
3 tablespoons water
1 teaspoon sesame oil

MARINADE
½ egg white, beaten
1 tablespoon dark soy sauce
1 tablespoon rice wine
1 teaspoon cornstarch

In a bowl, mix marinade. Clean chicken and dry with paper towels. Cut chicken lengthwise into ½-inch-wide strips, then cut again crosswise into ½-inch pieces and marinate for 20 to 30 minutes. Wipe clean and remove tips and seeds of dried red peppers. Use scissors to cut diagonally into ½-inch-long pieces or leave them whole. Mince ginger and garlic. In a small bowl, combine seasoning sauce.

Heat a wok or large skillet over high heat until hot; add oil and heat until hot. Toss in dried red peppers, pressing them into the oil until they turn dark. Add ginger and garlic and stir-fry for about 10 seconds. Add the chicken and stir-fry until the pieces are white and firm (about 2 minutes), then add the seasoning sauce and stir until it thickens. Keep warm. Bring a large pot of water to a boil and cook the broccoli florets for about 20 seconds. Drain into a colander. Pour the chicken onto a platter and decorate the florets around the chicken.

Serves 3 to 4.

LEMON CHICKEN
檸檬雞

When I was growing up in Taiwan, my mother did mostly stir-frying, steaming, and braising for our meals. This Cantonese dish is normally deep-fried; I was introduced to it after I immigrated to this country in the mid-1960s. I use a pan-frying method to cut down the fat content, but I still enjoy this succulent chicken. This is one of the rare dishes in Chinese cuisine that uses lemon. It puzzles me that in America an innocent lemon is used to describe an unsatisfactory purchase!

INGREDIENTS
1 pound boneless and skinless chicken
   breasts
½ cup flour
2 to 4 tablespoons oil
1 small lemon, thinly sliced
Lettuce leaves

SEASONING SAUCE
¼ cup lemon juice
¼ cup sugar
¼ cup chicken stock
2 teaspoons cornstarch
1 teaspoon sesame oil

MARINADE
1 tablespoon rice wine
1 tablespoon soy sauce
Dash white pepper

In a bowl, mix marinade. Put each breast between pieces of plastic wrap and pound to about ¼-inch thickness. Make very small cuts around edges of breasts to prevent curling. Place in a bowl, add the marinade ingredients, and toss lightly to coat. Marinate for at least 30 minutes (or refrigerate for up to 4 hours). In a small bowl, combine seasoning sauce.

Remove chicken pieces from the marinade. Carefully dredge the chicken pieces in flour. Heat a wok or large skillet, add oil, and heat to 325 degrees. Pan-fry chicken 2 minutes on each side or until brown. Remove the chicken to a plate and keep warm in the oven.

Add the lemon slices and seasoning sauce in the same wok or skillet on medium-high heat until sugar dissolves. Keep the sauce warm.

Take the chicken out of the oven and place it on a platter lined with lettuce leaves. Pour the sauce over the chicken.

Serves 2 to 3.

MINCED CHICKEN WITH LETTUCE WRAP
生菜包雞鬆

The original recipe called for a squab, but I have substituted chicken breast. Preparation of this interesting and delicious dish requires a lot of labor, so you should get your family or friends to help out. I guarantee that they will be very impressed with your culinary skills.

INGREDIENTS

½ pound boneless and skinless chicken
  breasts
5 ounces lean pork, diced
½ cup ham, diced
6 medium dried Chinese mushrooms, diced
1 small onion, diced
½ cup water chestnuts, diced
½ cup bamboo shoots, diced
½ cup cucumber, diced
2 cups oil
2 to 3 ounces thin rice noodles
24 lettuce leaves

SEASONING SAUCE

3 tablespoons soy sauce
1 teaspoon salt
¼ cup chicken stock
1 teaspoon cornstarch
⅛ teaspoon white pepper

MARINADE

1½ teaspoons soy sauce
½ teaspoon salt
2 teaspoons rice wine
2 teaspoons cornstarch

In a bowl, mix marinade. Soak mushrooms in hot water for 20 minutes. Discard the water and squeeze the mushrooms dry. Cut off and discard mushroom stems, then cut each cap into ¼-inch dice. Dice chicken, pork, ham, and all vegetables into ¼-inch pieces. Marinate chicken and pork for 20 to 30 minutes. Wash lettuce leaves and let them dry. Cut into round shapes. In a small bowl, combine seasoning sauce.

Heat a wok or large skillet over high heat until hot; add 2 cups oil, heat to about 375 degrees, and deep-fry the rice noodles, a little at a time, until they puff up. Remove and drain. Place on a platter and crush with a fork or chopsticks. Leaving ¼ cup oil in the wok, stir-fry chicken and pork for 1 to 2 minutes. Remove and set aside.

Return the wok or skillet to the heat, add 3 tablespoons of oil, and heat until hot. Stir-fry ham, mushrooms, onion, water chestnuts, bamboo shoots, and cucumber. After 1 minute add chicken, pork, and seasoning sauce. Stir-fry over high heat until the meat and vegetables are evenly coated with seasoning sauce. Serve in lettuce leaves, topped with puffed noodles and meat-and-vegetables mixture.

Serves 4 to 5.

PEKING DUCK
北京鴨

In China, Peking Duck usually is served at formal dinners or banquets. Ducks bred for this dish are kept in small, individual cages and fed a special grain mixture that quickly fattens them. Traditionally, when preparing the duck, the whole head is left intact. Air is pumped into the body, and the duck is hung in a cool place for several days to dry the skin. Since duck sold in American supermarkets lacks a head and neck, I use a fan to blow-dry the hanging body. In September 2001, my family and I visited the noted Quanjude Restaurant in Beijing, which specializes in Peking Duck.

INGREDIENTS
1 duck (about 4 to 5 pounds), fresh or
  frozen
2 whole green onions, smashed
3 slices ginger, smashed
3 tablespoons rice wine
½ cup honey

FOR SERVING
20 green onion brushes*
20 Mandarin pancakes (see page 136)
Hoisin sauce

Defrost the duck and clean. Use a chopstick to stretch the wing ends apart from the body. With a steel S-hook through the neck, hang the duck to dry in front of an electric fan for about 3½ hours.

Bring 6 cups of water to a boil in a large deep pot and add green onions, ginger, rice wine, and honey. Holding the duck by the hook over the pot, continuously ladle the boiling water and honey mixture over the duck for 2 to 3 minutes. Hang the duck in front of an electric fan and dry for another 4 hours.

Roast the duck on a rack, breast side down, in a 350-degree oven for 1½ hours. (To avoid burning the wings and legs, cover them with aluminum foil; remove the foil 20 minutes before roasting time is finished.) After 45 minutes, turn once. When the duck is removed, the skin should be golden brown and crispy. First slice all of the duck skin and then the meat into thin pieces.

On a pancake spread 1 teaspoon of hoisin sauce with a green onion brush; place onion brush and several slices of duck skin and meat on the pancake. Roll up the pancake and eat.

Serves 3 to 4.

*To make green onion brushes: Trim the root and cut off the green top, leaving 3 to 4 inches of firm stalk. Holding stalk firmly, make four crossing cuts 1 inch deep in one end. Repeat at other end. Place brushes in ice water for several hours. Before serving duck, remove brushes from ice water and shake off water.

SICHUAN DUCK
香酥鴨

If you ask me which is my favorite, Peking Duck or Sichuan Duck, I will tell you that I am really fond of the latter. Many people assume that all food from Sichuan is highly seasoned and spicy, but there are many good dishes that are not spicy at all. I just love to eat the crunchy piece of bone like a potato chip, and the meat is so flavorful and aromatic. When you steam the duck for 3 hours, make sure you have boiling water handy, as you will need to replenish it occasionally.

INGREDIENTS
1 duck (about 4 to 5 pounds), fresh or frozen
2 teaspoons Sichuan peppercorns
2 tablespoons kosher salt
1 teaspoon five-spice powder
5 slices fresh ginger, crushed
3 whole green onions, crushed
1 tablespoon soy sauce
4 to 5 cups oil
2 tablespoons flour
Lotus leaf buns (see page 135)

Wash and rinse the duck well and dry with paper towels. Cut off the excess fat and extra skin around the neck area, then remove the neck and the giblets from the cavity. Lay the duck breast side up and press down hard on the breast with palms of your hands to break the rib bone and backbone.

Put the Sichuan peppercorns and salt in a wok or frying pan over medium heat and stir-fry without oil for 5 to 6 minutes, stirring constantly. Let cool and add five-spice powder. Rub this mixture outside and inside the duck. Insert the ginger and green onions inside the cavity. Cover the duck and place in a refrigerator overnight.

The next day, remove the duck from refrigerator and drain off any liquid. In a large steamer lined with a damp cloth, place the duck breast side up and steam for 3 hours. Remove the duck from the steamer and let it cool off completely on a plate. Brush off the peppercorns and discard the ginger and green onions. Blot dry with paper towels. Then brush the duck all over with soy sauce and allow to dry for another 4 hours in the refrigerator. Remove the duck from the refrigerator one hour before deep-frying.

Heat a wok or large deep fryer over high heat for 1 minute. Add the oil and heat to 375 degrees. Sprinkle the flour to coat the duck and set it aside while you are heating the oil. Fry the duck 3 minutes each side until brown; remove the duck to a large plate. Reheat the oil again to 375 degrees and deep-fry the duck for another 2 minutes until golden brown and crispy. Cut the duck into small pieces through the skin and bone. Serve with hot lotus leaf buns. Sprinkle with salt and toasted Sichuan peppercorn powder if desired.

Serves 4 to 5.

SLICED CHICKEN WITH ASSORTED VEGETABLES
四季雞

Even though I came from a middle class family in Taiwan, chicken was seldom served at our meals. Chicken cost a lot more than pork when I was young; therefore, eating chicken was a rare occasion in the Lin family! You can use any kind of vegetables you like when you prepare this dish. I often use canned straw mushrooms and young baby corn. I usually serve this dish with fried rice or curried rice.

INGREDIENTS

1 pound boneless and skinless chicken breasts
4 ounces fresh mushrooms, sliced
¼ pound fresh snow peas
1 carrot, sliced
1 cup bamboo shoots or water chestnuts, sliced
1 teaspoon fresh ginger, minced
1 teaspoon fresh garlic, minced
4 tablespoons oil

SEASONING SAUCE

2 tablespoons oyster sauce
1 tablespoon rice wine
½ teaspoon salt
½ teaspoon sugar
¼ teaspoon white pepper
¼ cup chicken stock
2 teaspoons cornstarch
2 teaspoons sesame oil

MARINADE

½ egg white, beaten
½ teaspoon salt
1 tablespoon rice wine
1 teaspoon cornstarch

In a bowl, mix marinade. Cut chicken with the grain into 2-inch-wide strips. Then cut crosswise against the grain into ⅛-inch slices and marinate for 20 to 30 minutes. Wipe mushrooms clean with wet towel or wet cloth; slice the mushrooms if too large. String the snow peas; dip in boiling water for 15 seconds and drain. Peel and slice carrot diagonally into ⅛-inch pieces. Slice the bamboo shoots or water chestnuts. Mince ginger and garlic. In a small bowl, combine seasoning sauce.

Heat a wok or large skillet over high heat until hot; add oil and heat until hot. Add ginger and garlic; stir-fry for about 10 seconds. Add the chicken and stir-fry until the pieces are white and firm (about 2 minutes). Then add mushrooms, snow peas, carrot, and bamboo shoots or water chestnuts and cook for another minute. Add seasoning sauce. Stir until chicken and vegetables are coated with sauce and serve.

Serves 3 to 4.

SMOKED CHICKEN
燻雞

This dish is great as an appetizer. If you use a wire rack to smoke the chicken, as I describe below, I'm afraid that you will have to discard the rack after the smoking is done, as it would be very difficult to clean. Instead of a rack, I usually use three empty food cans which have been opened at both ends. When you are ready to smoke, place the chicken on top of the three cans. After the chicken is smoked, just throw the cans away, along with the aluminum foil or pie pan mentioned in the instructions below.

INGREDIENTS
1 chicken (about 3 pounds)
1 tablespoon salt
½ cup brown sugar
2 tablespoons tea leaves

COOKING SAUCE
1 cup soy sauce
1 stick cinnamon
1 teaspoon Sichuan peppercorns
1 tablespoon dried orange peels
2 whole green onions, smashed
3 slices ginger, smashed
1 tablespoon sugar
4 cups water

GARLIC SAUCE
1 tablespoon garlic, minced
1 tablespoon soy sauce
1 tablespoon sesame oil

Wash chicken and dry well inside and outside with paper towels. Rub chicken outside with salt. Place chicken in covered container or wrap completely in a Ziploc bag and store in refrigerator for at least 6 hours or overnight.

Combine cooking sauce in a deep pot and heat to boiling point. Boil for 3 minutes to bring out the flavor. Turn heat to medium-high, place chicken in pot breast side down, and cook for 10 minutes. Then turn the chicken over and cook for another 40 minutes. Baste occasionally. Remove chicken from pot and let it cool off and air-dry for 10 to 15 minutes.

Cover bottom of a Dutch oven or wide heavy pot with heavy aluminum foil or place an aluminum pie pan inside the pot. Turn heat to medium-high and put in brown sugar and tea leaves. When sugar begins to melt, turn heat to medium-low. Place chicken on a wire rack over brown sugar and tea leaves. Cover the pot tightly with a lid. Cover lid with a damp cloth and place inverted iron skillet on damp cloth to prevent smoke from escaping from pot. Smoke chicken for about 20 minutes, until it turns golden brown.

Remove the chicken from the pot, de-bone it, and cut into bite-sized pieces. Place on serving platter and pour the garlic sauce over it. Serve hot or cold.

Serves 3 to 4.

SOY SAUCE CHICKEN
醬油雞

When I was a youngster in Taiwan, we only ate chicken on special occasions like Chinese New Year. We didn't own a refrigerator, but this salty chicken dish would keep for days in the winter. You can enjoy this dish hot or cold.

INGREDIENTS
1 chicken (about 3 pounds)
1 tablespoon sesame oil (optional)
2 whole green onions, minced or chopped

COOKING SAUCE
½ cup dark soy sauce
4 slices fresh ginger, smashed
2 tablespoons rice wine
1 whole star anise
  or 8 sections star anise
1 cup broken rock sugar
  or ½ cup sugar
2 cups water
1 whole green onion, smashed

Clean chicken and dry with paper towels. Set aside. In a large pot, combine cooking sauce and heat to boiling point. Put in chicken, breast side down. Cover and cook for 10 minutes. Lower heat and turn chicken over. Cook about 20 more minutes per pound, basting occasionally. After chicken is cooked, remove from sauce, leaving sauce in pot. Brush chicken with sesame oil (optional). Cut chicken through the bone into 1-inch pieces. Arrange chicken pieces on a platter and pour cooking sauce over them. Garnish with green onion. Serve hot or cold.

Serves 3 to 4.

Note: If you prefer a salty taste, after the chicken is three-quarters cooked, turn heat to medium-high and baste chicken frequently for 10 to 15 minutes until the chicken is dark brown and only 1 cup of the liquid remains.

WALNUT CHICKEN
核桃雞

This dish has been voted by my students as one of their all-time favorites. There are many ways to make Walnut Chicken, and over the years I have tried to improve the flavor and simplify the preparation. One trick I have discovered is this: Put the uncooked chicken in the refrigerator for one hour to prevent the walnuts and sesame seeds from falling off when pan-frying. This dish can be made ahead of time and reheated in the microwave. The chicken remains tender and moist.

INGREDIENTS
1 pound boneless chicken (breasts or
   thighs)
½ cup flour
1 egg, well beaten with 1 tablespoon water
1 cup walnuts, finely chopped
½ cup toasted sesame seeds
8 tablespoons oil for pan-frying

MARINADE
2 tablespoons soy sauce
1 tablespoon rice wine
1 teaspoon sesame oil
2 teaspoons garlic, minced
2 teaspoons ginger, minced
⅛ teaspoon toasted Sichuan peppercorn
   powder (see page 169)

DIPPING SAUCE (OPTIONAL)
¼ cup chicken stock
2 tablespoons soy sauce
1 tablespoon rice wine
2 teaspoons sugar
1 teaspoon sesame oil
1 teaspoon rice vinegar
2 tablespoons green onion, minced

Put each chicken breast between pieces of plastic wrap and pound to about ¼-inch thickness. Make very small cuts around edges of breasts to prevent curling. Place in a bowl, add the marinade ingredients, and toss lightly to coat. Marinate for at least 30 minutes (or refrigerate for up to 4 hours). Mix chopped walnuts and sesame seeds.

Remove chicken pieces from the marinade. Carefully dredge the chicken pieces in flour. Dip the chicken in the egg mixture, letting any excess drip off. Dredge the chicken in the walnut and sesame seed mixture, coating each side completely.

Heat a wok or large skillet, add oil, and heat to 325 degrees. Pan-fry chicken 2 minutes on each side or until brown. You can serve the walnut chicken as a whole piece or cut up into small pieces and served with or without dipping sauce.

Serves 3 to 4 as main course, or 6 as an appetizer.

Seafood

FILLET OF FISH WITH FERMENTED BLACK BEANS
豆豉魚片

When we lived in Tainan, Taiwan, we ate a whole fish at lunch and at dinner. Fillet of fish was seldom served at our dining table. Since my father was the head of our household, the fish head always pointed toward him. When we had a guest, my mother would place the fish with the head facing our guest. This custom also applied to chicken or duck; that is why when we purchased fowl the head was always attached. Nowadays, in my local Chinese markets where I live, I still can buy whole fish and chicken with the head intact.

INGREDIENTS
1 pound fillet of fish (flounder or sole)
2 tablespoons fermented black beans, chopped
2 teaspoons ginger, minced
2 teaspoons garlic, minced
1 to 2 dried red peppers, chopped or ½ to 1 teaspoon fresh hot chili pepper, chopped
¼ cup country ham, chopped
1 whole green onion, chopped
3 tablespoons oil

SEASONING SAUCE
1 cup chicken stock
2 teaspoons cornstarch
2 tablespoons rice wine
½ teaspoon salt
2 teaspoons sesame oil
¼ teaspoon white pepper

MARINADE
1 egg white, beaten
1 tablespoon rice wine
½ tablespoon cornstarch
⅛ teaspoon white pepper

In a bowl, mix marinade. Pat the fillets with paper towels until dry. Cut each fillet into 1½-inch pieces and marinate for 20 to 30 minutes. Chop fermented black beans coarsely. Mince ginger and garlic. Chop red peppers, ham, and green onion. Grease a heatproof shallow bowl or 9-inch pie pan. In a small bowl, combine seasoning sauce.

Place the marinated fillet on the shallow bowl or pie pan, sprinkle the chopped ham on top of fish, and steam 5 minutes over high heat. While the fillet is being steamed, heat a wok or large skillet over high heat until hot; add 2 tablespoons of oil and heat until hot. Add the fermented black beans, ginger, garlic, and red peppers or chili pepper and stir-fry for a few seconds. Add the seasoning sauce and stir until the sauce is glazy and smooth.

Remove the fillets from the steamer, carefully pour off the liquid in the fish container, then pour the glazy sauce over the fish. Turn each piece gently but quickly. Sprinkle the green onion and 1 tablespoon of very hot oil over the top of the fish and serve at once.

Serves 2 to 3.

FISH ROLLED IN TOFU SHEET
糖醋魚卷

You can use various kinds of fish for this dish: for example, sea bass, red snapper, salmon, or flounder. Since only half the egg white is needed for the marinade, you can use the other half to seal the fish rolls.

INGREDIENTS
10 ounces firm fish fillet, such as sea bass
    or red snapper
1 large round frozen tofu sheet
3 tablespoons green onion, chopped
2 teaspoons ginger, minced
2 teaspoons garlic, minced
½ egg white, beaten
5 tablespoons oil

SEASONING SAUCE
5 tablespoons sugar
3 tablespoons white vinegar
2 tablespoons ketchup
1 tablespoon rice wine
7 tablespoons fish stock or chicken stock
½ teaspoon salt
2 teaspoons cornstarch
1 teaspoon sesame oil

MARINADE
½ egg white, beaten
¼ teaspoon salt
1 tablespoon rice wine
1 teaspoon sesame oil
½ teaspoon white pepper
1 tablespoon green onion, minced
1 teaspoon ginger juice (see page 165)

In a bowl, mix marinade. Cut the fish into thin slices and marinate for 20 to 30 minutes. Chop green onion; mince ginger and garlic. In a medium-sized bowl, combine seasoning sauce.

Bring the frozen tofu sheet to room temperature and keep it moist. Cut the sheet into 8 wedge-shaped pieces. Divide the marinated fish slices into 8 portions. Place each portion on the wide end of the tofu wedge, 1 inch from the edge. With your hands, begin to roll into a cylinder about 4 to 5 inches long. Bring the two end flaps up over the top of the enclosed filling and press gently. Then continue to roll to the far point to form a neat roll. Moisten the tip with beaten egg white and close the flap. Place on plate sealed edge down. Proceed with rest of filling and finish the 8 rolls.

Heat a 9-inch skillet over medium-low heat until hot. Add 4 tablespoons of oil. When oil is hot, add fish rolls without allowing them to overlap. Pan-fry both sides until brown (about 4 minutes each side). Remove the fish rolls to a platter and keep them warm.

Heat a wok or small skillet over medium heat until hot; add 1 tablespoon of oil and heat until hot. Stir-fry the ginger and garlic for about 10 seconds. Add the seasoning sauce and cook, stirring until sauce boils and thickens. Pour the sauce over the fish rolls and sprinkle with chopped green onions.

Serves 3 to 4.

PAPER-WRAPPED SHRIMP
紙包蝦

Traditionally, this dish was made by deep-frying in oil, mainly because Chinese kitchens didn't have ovens. Not only does deep-frying add extra calories, it's also a time-consuming way to cook this dish. I use the oven method instead. It's easy, and the taste is great, too. You can substitute chicken, beef, or pork for shrimp.

INGREDIENTS

$1^1/_3$ pounds large shrimp
1 stalk of leek
1 medium carrot, sliced
$^1/_4$ pound snow peas, sliced
8 water chestnuts, sliced
22 to 24 $7^1/_2$-inch x $7^1/_2$-inch parchment
    paper squares
2 tablespoons sesame oil
$^1/_4$ cup Chinese parsley leaves

MARINADE

1 egg white
2 tablespoons rice wine
2 tablespoons soy sauce
1 teaspoon ginger juice (see page 165)
1 teaspoon cornstarch
1 teaspoon rice vinegar
1 teaspoon sugar
$^1/_2$ teaspoon salt

In a bowl, mix marinade. Wash shrimp if desired. Shell shrimp and remove the black vein. Dry with paper towels and marinate for 20 to 30 minutes. Cut off the white part of leek and save it for other cooking. Slice carrot, snow peas, and water chestnuts. Bring 4 cups water to a boil and parboil the green part of the leek, carrot, and snow peas for 20 seconds. Remove and drain. Using your fingers, tear the leek into $^1/_4$-inch x 7-inch-long strings and set them aside. These are the strings that will be used for tying the package.

Take a pre-cut piece of parchment paper and brush lightly with sesame oil. Place one piece each of chestnut, carrot, and snow pea in center of square. Top with 1 marinated shrimp and a few Chinese parsley leaves. Pull all of the edges together to the center and form a bag. Tie it with a leek string and repeat until all packets are made. Place all packets on a baking sheet, one inch apart, and bake in a pre-heated oven (425 degrees) for 10 minutes. To eat, cut the leek string off with your fork or chopsticks and spread out the paper.

Makes 22 to 24 bags.

SHRIMP WITH LOBSTER SAUCE
蝦龍糊

Please don't get too excited thinking that you will enjoy some lobster in this dish. In fact, I had never heard of this dish until I came to this country. Since lobster isn't an everyday affordable dish, the person who devised this shrimp recipe was smart enough to use the same kind of sauce made for lobster. This is a salty dish with a very tasty sauce, so it is best served with plain boiled rice.

INGREDIENTS
1 pound medium shrimp
½ pound ground pork
1½ tablespoons fermented black beans,
   chopped
1 teaspoon ginger, minced
1 teaspoon garlic, minced
3 tablespoons oil
1 tablespoon cornstarch and 1 tablespoon
   water to make a paste
1 egg, well beaten
1 whole green onion, chopped
   or 2 to 3 tablespoons Chinese parsley,
   chopped

SEASONING SAUCE
2 tablespoons soy sauce
¼ teaspoon salt
½ teaspoon sugar
1 cup chicken stock

MARINADE
1 tablespoon rice wine
½ tablespoon cornstarch

In a bowl, mix marinade. Wash shrimp if desired. Shell shrimp and remove the black vein. Dry with paper towels and marinate for 20 to 30 minutes. Chop fermented black beans coarsely. Mince ginger and garlic. In a small bowl, combine seasoning sauce.

Heat a wok or large skillet over high heat until hot; add 2 tablespoons of oil and heat until hot. Stir-fry the shrimp until pink and firm. Remove and keep warm. Add 1 tablespoon of oil in the wok. Stir-fry fermented black beans, ginger, and garlic for a few seconds. Then add the pork and stir-fry for another minute. Add seasoning sauce and bring to a boil. Cover and simmer for 1 minute. Stir in cornstarch paste and shrimp. Add egg until it is cooked. Garnish with chopped green onion or Chinese parsley.

Serves 3 to 4.

SHRIMP WITH SUGAR PEAS OR SNOW PEAS
蝦仁炒雪豆

When we were growing up in Taiwan, shrimp was served only at banquets or on special occasions. This dish is light and easy to prepare. The pink shrimp and green vegetables are a great color combination. You will love this dish if you don't like highly seasoned or spicy food.

INGREDIENTS
1 pound shrimp
2 cups fresh sugar peas or snow peas
6 medium dried Chinese mushrooms, shredded
1 whole green onion, chopped
1 teaspoon ginger, minced
1 teaspoon garlic, minced
4 tablespoons oil

SEASONING SAUCE
1 tablespoon rice wine
½ teaspoon salt
1 tablespoon sesame oil
½ teaspoon white pepper
1 teaspoon sugar
2 teaspoons cornstarch
¼ cup chicken stock

MARINADE
1 egg white, beaten
1 tablespoon oil
½ teaspoon salt
1 tablespoon rice wine

In a bowl, mix marinade. Wash shrimp if desired. Shell shrimp and remove the black vein. Dry with paper towels and marinate for 20 to 30 minutes. String the sugar peas. Bring 4 cups water to a boil in a deep pot, put in sugar peas, and parboil about 2 minutes. (If using snow peas instead of sugar peas, parboil for about 15 seconds.) Remove sugar peas and drain. Soak mushrooms in hot water for 20 minutes. Discard the water and squeeze the mushrooms dry. Cut off and discard mushroom stems, then cut each cap into ¼-inch strips. Chop green onion; mince ginger and garlic. In a small bowl, combine seasoning sauce.

Heat a wok or large skillet over high heat until hot; add 4 tablespoons of oil and heat until hot. Stir-fry the chopped green onion, ginger, and garlic for a few seconds. Scatter in the shrimp and stir-fry until pink (about 1 to 2 minutes). Add sugar peas and mushrooms to the shrimp. Stir the vegetables until they are thoroughly heated, pour in seasoning sauce, and stir thoroughly. Remove to a plate and serve.

Serves 3 to 4.

SICHUAN BRAISED SHRIMP
乾燒明蝦

Even though we seldom ate shrimp at home in Taiwan, we learned at a very young age that it is definitely tastier with the shell on. We enjoyed the shrimp by using our tongues to skillfully remove the shells. My American husband still prefers to eat shrimp without the shell. The sauce in this dish goes well with plain boiled rice.

INGREDIENTS

1½ pounds large shrimp
1 tablespoon ginger, minced
1 tablespoon garlic, minced
1 whole green onion, minced
7 tablespoons oil
2 teaspoons hot bean sauce
¼ cup tomato ketchup
1 tablespoon cornstarch and 1 tablespoon
   water to make a paste
1 teaspoon sesame oil

SEASONING SAUCE

3 tablespoons rice wine
1 teaspoon salt
2 teaspoons sugar
1 cup chicken stock

Wash shrimp if desired. Cut each shrimp down the back and de-vein it. Do not remove the shell. Dry with paper towels. Mince ginger, garlic, and green onion. In small bowl, combine seasoning sauce.

Heat a wok or large skillet over high heat until hot; add 5 tablespoons of oil and heat until hot. Drop in shrimp and cook until both sides turn pink (about 2 minutes). Add seasoning sauce and cook over high heat for about 3 minutes. Remove the shrimp and save the shrimp stock in the wok.

In a small pot or small frying pan, heat 2 tablespoons of oil and stir-fry ginger, garlic, green onion, and hot bean sauce for 30 seconds. Add to the shrimp stock and cook over high heat until the stock is reduced to about two-thirds the original amount. Return the shrimp to the wok and cook another 30 seconds. Add tomato ketchup and cook another 30 seconds. Stir in cornstarch paste until sauce thickens and shrimp is evenly coated. Sprinkle shrimp with 1 teaspoon sesame oil just before serving.

Serves 3 to 4.

STEAMED SEA BASS WITH CREAM SAUCE
白汁蒸全魚

When I was growing up in Taiwan, where seafood is abundant, whole fish was served at lunch and at dinner every day in our house. As a child, I often accompanied my mother to the market and helped her select the fresh fish. I learned at a very young age how to scale and clean the body cavity, leaving the head and tail intact.

INGREDIENTS
1 sea bass, with head and tail, about 1½ pounds
1 teaspoon ginger, minced
1 whole green onion, chopped
¼ cup bamboo shoots, diced
¼ cup straw mushrooms, diced
¼ cup ham, diced
1 tablespoon oil
¼ cup fresh soybeans
2 teaspoons cornstarch and 2 teaspoons water to make a paste
1 egg white, beaten

SEASONING SAUCE
Juice from fish and cream to make 1 cup
¼ teaspoon salt
½ teaspoon white pepper
1 teaspoon sesame oil

MARINADE
1 teaspoon salt
1 tablespoon rice wine
2 whole green onions, smashed
4 slices ginger, smashed

In a bowl, mix marinade. Clean and scale the fish, leaving the head and tail on (some fish markets will do this for you). Rinse and dry with paper towels. With a cleaver of sharp knife, score each side of the fish 3 times diagonally, about 1 inch apart and ¼ inch deep. Marinate the fish for 20 to 30 minutes. Mince ginger and chop green onion. Dice bamboo shoots, straw mushrooms, and ham.

Put two pairs crossed chopsticks on a heatproof shallow bowl and place the fish on top of the chopsticks, so the steam can reach the bottom of the fish. Place bowl in a steamer and steam the fish for 15 minutes. Heat a wok or large skillet over high heat until hot; add oil and heat until hot. Stir-fry the ginger and green onions for about 30 seconds; add the bamboo shoots, straw mushrooms, ham, and soybeans and stir-fry briskly for 2 minutes. Set aside and keep warm.

Remove the bowl and fish from the steamer and carefully pour out the juice into a cup. Remove the green onions and ginger from the juice, then add cream to make 1 cup. Keep fish warm in steamer, if desired. In a small bowl, combine seasoning sauce. Bring the seasoning sauce to a slow boil, then turn heat to low. Add vegetables and ham mixture. Add the cornstarch paste to the sauce and stir until the sauce is smooth. Stir in the beaten egg white slowly until nicely blended. Pour the sauce over the fish and serve.

Serves 2 to 3.

STEAMED WHOLE FISH
蒸全魚

In my recipe for Fillet of Fish with Fermented Black Beans, I mentioned that it is a tradition in China to serve fish whole. Not only does the fish head face the head of the household or the honored guest, but the whole fish symbolizes completion, perfection, and harmony. Even Chinese people living in this country still prefer to eat the fish with the head on. I must say that fish definitely tastes superior when served with the bone.

INGREDIENTS
1 sea bass, with head and tail, about 1½
   pounds
½ teaspoon salt
1 tablespoon rice wine
¼ teaspoon black pepper
1 tablespoon fermented black beans,
   chopped
2 teaspoons ginger, minced
2 teaspoons garlic, minced
2 dried red peppers, chopped
2 whole green onions, chopped
1 tablespoon oil
1 tablespoon cornstarch and 1 tablespoon
   water to make a paste

SEASONING SAUCE
1 cup chicken stock
¼ teaspoon salt
2 teaspoons rice wine
2 tablespoons soy sauce
2 teaspoons sugar
1 teaspoon sesame oil

Wash the bass under cold water and pat it dry inside and out with paper towels. With a cleaver of sharp knife, score each side of the fish 3 times diagonally, about 1 inch apart and ¼ inch deep. Then rub the fish with salt, rice wine, and black pepper over the inside and outside.

Put two pairs crossed chopsticks on a heatproof shallow bowl and place the fish on top of the chopsticks, so the steam can reach the bottom of the fish. Place bowl in a steamer and steam the fish for 15 minutes. Chop fermented black beans coarsely. Mince ginger and garlic. Chop red peppers, and green onions. In a small bowl, combine seasoning sauce.

Heat a wok or large skillet over high heat until hot; add oil and heat until hot. Stir-fry the fermented black beans, ginger, garlic, red peppers, and green onions for about 20 seconds. Add the seasoning sauce until well blended. Turn heat to low and slowly stir in cornstarch paste until the sauce thickens. Drain the water from the fish and remove the chopsticks. Pour the sauce over the fish and serve.

Serves 2 to 3.

SWEET AND SOUR FISH
糖醋魚片

I don't recall that my mother ever served us fillet of fish. Instead, every part of a whole fish was devoured in the Lin family. Since I came to this country and married a Caucasian, whole fish is hardly ever served in my family. In this recipe, you can substitute a whole fish (2 to 3 pounds) for the fillet. I guarantee that you will please your Chinese friends if you serve them whole fish.

INGREDIENTS
1 pound fillet of flounder
4 dried Chinese mushrooms, diced
2 teaspoons ginger, minced
2 teaspoons garlic, minced
1 medium tomato, diced
1 small onion, diced
3 cups oil for deep-frying
2 tablespoons green peas

BATTER
½ cup flour
½ cup cornstarch
⅓ cup water or less
½ teaspoon baking powder
¼ teaspoon salt
1 egg, well beaten

SEASONING SAUCE
6 tablespoons sugar
6 tablespoons rice vinegar
2 tablespoons ketchup
2 tablespoons soy sauce
1 teaspoon salt
2 tablespoons rice wine
1 cup chicken stock
2½ tablespoons cornstarch and 2½ tablespoons water to make a paste
2 teaspoons sesame oil

MARINADE
¼ teaspoon salt
1 tablespoon rice wine
Dash of white pepper

In a bowl, mix marinade. Dry fish well with paper towels. Cut fish into 1½-inch or 2-inch pieces. Marinate for 20 to 30 minutes. Soak mushrooms in hot water for 20 minutes. Discard the water and squeeze the mushrooms dry. Cut off and discard mushroom stems, then cut each cap into ¼-inch dice. Mince ginger and garlic.

Bring a pot of water to a boil; immerse the tomato in boiling water for 1 minute, then immediately in cold water, then drain and peel. Cut the tomato in half and gently squeeze it to remove excess juice; seed with a small spoon. Cut onion and tomato into ¼-inch dice. Put all vegetables in one bowl. Mix batter in another bowl and coat the fish thoroughly with batter. In a small bowl, combine seasoning sauce.

Heat a wok or large skillet over high heat, add the oil, and heat to about 375 degrees. Deep-fry the fish until slightly brown. Remove and drain. Heat the oil to 400 degrees and deep-fry the fish once more until crispy. Remove, drain, and keep warm in oven. Heat 2 tablespoons of oil and stir-fry ginger, garlic, mushrooms, tomato, onion, and green peas. Stir in seasoning sauce until it thickens and the vegetables are glazed. Pour over the fish and serve at once.

Serves 3 to 4.

Egg and Tofu

EGG FU YUNG
芙蓉蛋

Fu yung in Chinese means hibiscus flower. In ancient China, a woman's face was described as being as beautiful as a hibiscus. This omelet is seen to be as colorful as that flower. This is a very famous Cantonese dish, which normally is deep-fried, but I use the stir-frying method.

INGREDIENTS

6 eggs, well beaten
½ teaspoon salt
3 dried Chinese mushrooms, shredded
1 cup ham or other cooked meat, shredded
½ cup bamboo shoots, shredded
½ cup green onion, shredded
½ cup carrots, shredded
1 cup bean sprouts
5 tablespoons oil

SEASONING SAUCE

1½ cups chicken stock (see page 18)
½ teaspoon salt
1 tablespoon soy sauce
1 tablespoon oyster sauce
1 tablespoon rice wine
1 teaspoon sesame oil
1½ tablespoons cornstarch
¼ cup soybeans

Beat eggs with salt in a large bowl and set aside. Soak mushrooms in hot water for 20 minutes. Discard the water and squeeze the mushrooms dry. Cut off and discard mushroom stems, then cut each cap into ¼-inch strips. Shred ham, bamboo shoots, green onion, and carrots.

Heat a wok or large skillet over high heat until hot; add 2 tablespoons of oil and heat until hot. Stir-fry mushrooms, ham, bamboo shoots, green onion, carrots, and bean sprouts for 2 minutes. Drain and let the meat and vegetable mixture cool. Add the mixture to the beaten eggs and mix well.

Heat 3 tablespoons of oil in a 10-inch non-stick frying pan. Pour in the egg mixture and cook like an omelet, lifting the cooked portion all around so the uncooked portion can flow underneath. Cook only until the egg mixture is softly set but still moist. I like to put the pan under the broiler for 1 minute or more. The face of the omelet should be set but not brown. Loosen the omelet with a spatula and slide it onto a platter. Keep warm.

Combine seasoning sauce in a small saucepan and cook over medium heat until the sauce thickens. Pour it over the omelet. You can cut the omelet into serving wedges, like a pie.

Serves 3 to 4.

MA-PO'S TOFU
麻婆豆腐

Ma in Chinese means pockmarked and po means old lady. I have been intrigued by this famous Sichuan dish ever since I was a child. This is a true story: In the 1860s, Mr. and Mrs. Chen owned a well-known restaurant in Chendu, capital of Sichuan Province. Mrs. Chen had bound feet and was a fantastic cook. Even though she wasn't a beautiful woman and was quite elderly, she created this spicy tofu dish that became extremely popular in China and around the world.

INGREDIENTS
1½ tubs (24 ounces) firm tofu
½ pound ground pork
1 teaspoon ginger, minced
1 teaspoon garlic, minced
2 teaspoons fermented black beans,
   chopped
1 whole green onion, chopped
4 tablespoons oil
1 tablespoon hot bean sauce
2 tablespoons dark soy sauce
½ teaspoon salt
1 teaspoon dried red pepper powder
¾ cup chicken stock
2 teaspoons cornstarch and 2 teaspoons
   water to make a paste
1 teaspoon sesame oil
¼ teaspoon toasted Sichuan peppercorn
   powder (see page 169)

MARINADE
1 teaspoon rice wine
1 teaspoon cornstarch
1 tablespoon dark soy sauce

In a bowl, mix marinade. Marinate ground pork for 20 to 30 minutes. Cut the tofu into ½-inch dice. Mince ginger and garlic. Chop black beans and green onion.

Heat a wok or large skillet over high heat until hot; add oil and heat until hot. Stir-fry ground pork well, then add ginger, garlic, fermented black beans, hot bean sauce, soy sauce, salt, and dried red pepper powder and stir-fry for 15 seconds. Add chicken stock and tofu and boil for 2 minutes. Slowly stir in cornstarch paste until mixture thickens, then sprinkle with green onion and sesame oil. Remove to a plate and sprinkle with toasted Sichuan peppercorn powder.

Serves 3 to 4.

MA-PO'S TOFU, VEGETARIAN
素麻婆豆腐

A lot of students at my tofu workshop are surprised to learn that tofu is often cooked with ground pork or ground beef. I created this dish by deleting the meat and increasing the tofu. If you are interested to know about the origin of this dish, please read about Ma-Po's Tofu on the previous page.

INGREDIENTS
2 tubs (32 ounces) firm tofu
1 teaspoon ginger, minced
1 teaspoon garlic, minced
2 teaspoons fermented black beans, chopped
1 whole green onion, chopped
2 tablespoons oil
1 tablespoon hot bean sauce
2 tablespoons dark soy sauce
½ teaspoon salt
1 teaspoon dried red pepper powder
¾ cup vegetable stock
2 teaspoons cornstarch and 2 teaspoons water to make a paste
1 teaspoon sesame oil
¼ teaspoon toasted Sichuan peppercorn powder (see page 169)

Cut the tofu into ½-inch dice. Mince ginger and garlic. Chop black beans and green onion.

Heat a wok or large skillet over high heat until hot; add oil and heat until hot. Stir-fry ginger, garlic, fermented black beans, hot bean sauce, soy sauce, salt, and dried red pepper powder for 15 seconds. Add vegetable stock and tofu and boil for 2 minutes. Slowly stir in cornstarch paste until mixture thickens, then sprinkle with green onion and sesame oil. Remove to a plate and sprinkle with toasted Sichuan peppercorn powder.

Serves 3 to 4.

SHREDDED TOFU SALAD
凉拌乾絲

Shredded tofu can be purchased either plain or seasoned. For this dish, I use the plain variety in my cooking classes to bring out the contrast with the celery and carrot. I also use plain or seasoned pressed tofu to make this dish; many of my students prefer pressed tofu to the shredded variety. You can use a shredder or food processor to shred the celery and carrot.

INGREDIENTS
8 ounces shredded tofu
1 cup celery, shredded
1 large carrot, shredded

SAUCE FOR SALAD
4 tablespoons soy sauce
4 tablespoons sesame oil
½ teaspoon salt
½ teaspoon white pepper
1 to 2 teaspoons chili oil

Shred celery and carrot. Bring 8 cups of water to a boil and add shredded tofu. Cook for 10 minutes. Drain and rinse in cold water. Drain again. Put shredded tofu, celery, and carrot on a platter. Add sauce. Toss well and serve.

Serves 2 to 3.

SMOKED TOFU SALAD
凉拌燻豆乾

Salad is not traditionally served with Chinese meals as it is in American cuisine. I created this dish so that my students can prepare it a day ahead of time. You can also use pressed tofu to make this salad.

INGREDIENTS
4 ounces smoked tofu, shredded
1½ cups carrot, shredded
1½ cups snow peas, shredded (about 3 ounces)
1 tablespoon dried shrimp, minced
1 tablespoon rice wine
1 tablespoon Sichuan preserved mustard stems, minced
2 tablespoons Chinese parsley, chopped
1 tablespoon toasted sesame seeds

SAUCE FOR SALAD
4 tablespoons soy sauce
4 tablespoons sesame oil
½ teaspoon salt

Shred smoked tofu, carrot, and snow peas. Soak dried shrimp in rice wine and 1 cup boiling water for 20 minutes. Mince the dried shrimp and Sichuan preserved mustard stems; chop the Chinese parsley.

Bring 8 cups water to a boil, add smoked tofu, then bring to a boil again. Add carrot and snow peas and parboil for 45 seconds. Remove and drain, then plunge into ice water and drain again.

Mix the sauce thoroughly and set aside. Place the shredded smoked tofu, carrot, and snow peas on a platter or in a bowl. Add minced shrimp, Sichuan preserved mustard stems, and Chinese parsley. Pour sauce over just before serving. Sprinkle sesame seeds on top.

Serves 2 to 3.

Note: You can add 1 to 2 teaspoons of chili oil to the sauce if you want this dish to be spicy.

STIR-FRIED MINCED VEGETABLES WITH PRESSED TOFU
豆腐乾鬆

You will love this dish even if you are not a vegetarian. The vegetables, along with the deep-fried rice stick noodles, are a unique and quite refreshing combination. If you cut the core out of the iceberg lettuce, the leaves are very easy to remove. The leftover oil can be used for refrying or stir-frying; I always use a coffee filter to remove impurities.

INGREDIENTS
4 ounces pressed tofu
4 medium dried Chinese mushrooms, diced
1 small carrot, diced
½ cup water chestnuts, diced
½ cup bamboo shoots, diced
½ cup cucumber, diced
15 or more lettuce leaves
2 cups oil
2 to 3 ounces rice stick noodles

SEASONING SAUCE
4 tablespoons soy sauce
1 teaspoon salt
½ cup vegetable stock
2 teaspoons cornstarch
½ teaspoon white pepper
2 teaspoons sesame oil

Soak mushrooms in hot water for 20 minutes. Discard the water and squeeze the mushrooms dry. Cut off and discard mushroom stems, then cut each cap into ¼-inch dice. Dice pressed tofu, carrot, water chestnuts, bamboo shoots, and cucumber into ¼-inch pieces. Wash lettuce leaves, pat dry, and cut into round shapes.

In a small bowl, combine seasoning sauce. Heat a wok or large skillet over high heat until hot. Add oil, heat to about 375 degrees, and deep-fry the rice noodles, a little at a time, until they puff up. Remove and drain. Place on a platter and crush with a fork or chopsticks.

Leaving ¼ cup oil in the wok, stir-fry all vegetables for 1 minute. Add seasoning sauce. Stir until all vegetables are coated with sauce. Pour the mixture over the crushed rice noodles. Serve on lettuce leaves.

Serves 4 to 5.

STIR-FRIED PRESSED TOFU, VEGETARIAN
炒乾絲

When I conduct my tofu workshop, I often have vegetarians in the classroom. So I prepare one dish cooked with pork and one without pork. For the latter, I replace oyster sauce with vegetarian mushroom sauce.

INGREDIENTS
8 ounces pressed tofu, shredded
½ cup Sichuan preserved mustard greens, shredded
½ cup green pepper, shredded
½ cup red pepper, shredded
1 whole green onion, shredded
2 teaspoons ginger, minced
2 teaspoons garlic, minced
4 tablespoons oil
Mandarin pancakes (optional, see page 136)
Hoisin sauce (optional)

SEASONING SAUCE
2 tablespoons vegetarian mushroom sauce
¼ teaspoon white pepper
1 teaspoon sesame oil
2 teaspoons cornstarch
¼ cup vegetable stock

Shred pressed tofu, mustard greens, green pepper, red pepper, and green onion. Mince ginger and garlic. In a small bowl, combine seasoning sauce.

Heat a wok or large skillet over high heat until hot; add oil and heat until hot. Stir-fry the ginger and garlic for a few seconds. Add pressed tofu, Sichuan mustard greens, green pepper, and red pepper and stir-fry until hot. Add seasoning sauce and stir thoroughly. Sprinkle green onion over top. If you like, brush a little hoisin sauce on a Mandarin pancake, roll up, and eat.

Serves 3 to 4.

STIR-FRIED PRESSED TOFU WITH PORK
豆腐乾炒肉

You can buy pressed tofu plain or seasoned in Asian supermarkets. I usually use the seasoned variety in my cooking classes and at home. You can also buy smoked pressed tofu if you wish. This dish can be made into a vegetarian dish by deleting the pork and using 8 ounces of pressed tofu (see previous recipe). If you prefer a spicy taste, simply add one to two teaspoons of fresh minced hot chili pepper with the minced ginger and garlic when stir-frying.

INGREDIENTS
4 ounces pressed tofu, shredded
4 ounces pork, shredded
½ cup Sichuan preserved mustard greens, shredded
½ cup green pepper, shredded
½ cup red pepper, shredded
1 whole green onion, shredded
2 teaspoons ginger, minced
2 teaspoons garlic, minced
4 tablespoons oil

SEASONING SAUCE
2 tablespoons oyster sauce
¼ teaspoon white pepper
1 teaspoon sesame oil
2 teaspoons cornstarch
¼ cup chicken stock
1 teaspoon sugar
1 tablespoon rice wine

MARINADE
1 teaspoon soy sauce
1 teaspoon cornstarch
1 teaspoon rice wine

In a bowl, mix marinade. Shred the pork and marinate for 20 to 30 minutes. Shred pressed tofu, mustard greens, green pepper, red pepper, and green onion. Mince ginger and garlic. In a small bowl, combine seasoning sauce.

Heat a wok or large skillet over high heat until hot; add oil and heat until hot. Stir-fry the ginger and garlic for a few seconds. Scatter in the pork and stir-fry briskly until it turns white. Add pressed tofu, Sichuan mustard greens, green pepper, and red pepper until hot. Add seasoning sauce and stir thoroughly. Sprinkle green onion over top and serve at once.

Serves 3 to 4.

STUFFED TOFU ROLLS
白頁卷

Soybeans aren't just for eating fresh; they're also used to make soy sauce, bean sauce, bean sprouts, and many other products. The fresh tofu skin used in this recipe is made from dehydrated soybeans and can be found in Chinese markets. Be aware that there are many different kinds of tofu skins, such as tofu sheets, which are usually frozen, and tofu sticks, which are usually dried.

INGREDIENTS
1 package (9 ounces) fresh tofu skins
½ pound pork, shredded
3 dried Chinese mushrooms, shredded
2 teaspoons baking soda
4 cups water
¼ cup bamboo shoots, shredded
¼ cup Sichuan preserved mustard stems, shredded
Shredded carrot and shredded onion

SEASONING SAUCE
1 cup beef stock
1 tablespoon cornstarch
½ teaspoon red pepper powder
2 teaspoons sesame oil

MARINADE
1 teaspoon soy sauce
1 teaspoon ginger, minced
1 whole green onion, minced
2 teaspoons sesame oil
1 small pickled hot pepper, minced

Soak fresh tofu skins in baking soda and water for 20 minutes. Rinse them well and cut each tofu skin into a 9½-inch x 9½-inch square. You will have a total of 5 sheets. Set aside and keep them moist.

In a bowl, mix marinade. Cut the pork with the grain into ⅛-inch thickness, then cut against the grain into 2-inch-long shreds and marinate for 20 to 30 minutes. Soak mushrooms in hot water for 20 minutes. Discard the water and squeeze the mushrooms dry. Cut off and discard mushroom stems, then cut each cap into ¼-inch strips. Shred the bamboo shoots and Sichuan preserved mustard stems. Add the mushrooms, bamboo shoots, and Sichuan preserved mustard stems to the pork. Divide this meat filling into 5 portions.

Place one portion of filling in a corner of a wrapper, 1 inch from the edge. With your hands, begin rolling into a cylinder about 4 inches long. Bring the two end flaps up over the top of the enclosed filling and press gently. Then continue to roll to the far point to form a neat roll.

Put the tofu rolls into a heatproof dish and steam them for 15 minutes. While the tofu rolls are being steamed, combine seasoning sauce in a small saucepan and cook in medium-high heat until it thickens. Drain the water from the heatproof dish and pour the sauce on top of the rolls. Garnish with shredded carrot and shredded onion.

Serves 3 to 4.

TOFU AND EGGPLANT WITH CURRY SAUCE
咖喱豆腐茄子

I created this dish for the tofu workshop that I teach because many of my students are vegetarians. Since tofu itself has little flavor, I use plenty of spices. The result is quite good. This dish should be served with plain boiled rice. Chinese people don't usually use lemon juice, but I think it really gives this dish some zest.

INGREDIENTS
1 tub (16 ounces) firm tofu
2 small Chinese eggplants, about 8 ounces, sliced
1 medium onion, sliced
2 teaspoons ginger, minced
2 teaspoons garlic, minced
2 to 3 tablespoons Chinese parsley, chopped
3 to 4 tablespoons oil
½ to 1 tablespoon curry paste
1 teaspoon ground chili paste
1 tablespoon fresh lemon juice

SEASONING SAUCE
1 can (13.5 ounces) coconut milk
2 whole cloves
1 stick cinnamon
½ teaspoon salt

Slice the tofu into 1½-inch x 1¼-inch pieces. Wash the eggplant and remove and discard the stems, then cut into thin slices. Slice onion, mince ginger and garlic, and chop Chinese parsley. In a small bowl, combine seasoning sauce.

Heat a wok or large skillet over high heat until hot; add oil and heat until hot. Stir-fry onion until soft (about 3 minutes). Add ginger, garlic, curry paste, and ground chili paste. Stir-fry another 30 seconds. Add eggplant and stir-fry another 4 minutes. Add the seasoning sauce and cook until it boils. Add the sliced tofu and turn the heat down; simmer for 5 minutes with a cover. Add the lemon juice and cook for another minute. Remove to a platter and sprinkle with chopped Chinese parsley.

Serves 3 to 4.

TOFU IN A POT
砂鍋豆腐

This one-dish meal, very filling and satisfying, can be served year round but is especially welcome on a cold winter's day. It should be cooked in a traditional Chinese earthenware pot made of sand and clay. This pot is fragile, so you must place a heatproof pad under it when simmering. I have found that a 2-quart saucepan is a good substitute for an earthenware pot. This dish can be prepared a day ahead and reheated in the microwave.

INGREDIENTS

1 tub (16 ounces) firm tofu
8 ounces boneless and skinless chicken
    (breasts or thighs), sliced
8 ounces napa cabbage
2 packages (1.3 ounces each) cellophane
    noodles
6 dried Chinese mushrooms
2 tablespoons country ham, sliced
4 whole green onions, chopped

1 tablespoon ginger, minced
1 tablespoon garlic, minced
2 tablespoons oil
1 tablespoon dried shrimp
3 cups chicken stock (see page 18)
1 teaspoon salt
½ teaspoon white pepper
2 tablespoons soybeans

Drain the tofu and slice it into 1½-inch x 1-inch x ¼-inch pieces. Wash cabbage and cut into ¾-inch strips; place the cabbage in the bottom of a 2-quart saucepan. Soak cellophane noodles in hot water until soft (about 10 to 12 minutes), then cut with scissors into shorter lengths (6 to 8 inches). Rinse and drain. Place the soft cellophane noodles over the cabbage. Spread sliced tofu carefully over cellophane noodles.

Cut chicken with the grain into 2-inch-wide strips. Then cut crosswise against the grain into ⅛-inch slices. Soak mushrooms in hot water for 20 minutes. Discard the water and squeeze the mushrooms dry. Cut off and discard mushroom stems, then cut each cap into ½-inch slices. Cut country ham into ½-inch slices. Lay sliced chicken, mushrooms, and ham on top of tofu. Chop green onions; mince ginger and garlic.

Heat a wok or large skillet over high heat until hot; add oil and heat until hot. Stir-fry green onions, ginger, garlic, and dried shrimp for about 20 seconds until fragrant. Add chicken stock, salt, and white pepper; cook until mixture boils. Pour mixture into saucepan containing tofu and bring to a boil, then simmer for 18 minutes with a cover. Sprinkle the soybeans on top of the tofu mixture and simmer another 2 minutes. Serve directly from the pot.

Serves 3 to 4.

TOFU IN A POT, MEATLESS
素砂鍋豆腐

This is a great wintertime one-dish meal. You can read more about this dish in the previous recipe. I have substituted white fish for the chicken and ham, and I use vegetable stock instead of chicken stock.

INGREDIENTS

1 tub (16 ounces) firm tofu
12 ounces firm white fish
8 ounces napa cabbage
2 packages (1.3 ounces each) cellophane
  noodles
6 dried Chinese mushrooms
4 whole green onions, chopped

1 tablespoon ginger, minced
1 tablespoon garlic, minced
2 tablespoons oil
1 tablespoon dried shrimp
3 cups vegetable stock
½ teaspoon white pepper
2 tablespoons soybeans

Drain the tofu and slice it into 1½-inch x 1-inch x ¼-inch pieces. Wash cabbage and cut into ¾-inch strips; place the cabbage in the bottom of a 2-quart saucepan. Soak cellophane noodles in hot water until soft (about 10 to 12 minutes) and then cut with scissors into shorter lengths (6 to 8 inches). Rinse and drain. Place the soft cellophane noodles over the cabbage. Spread sliced tofu carefully over cellophane noodles.

Cut the fish into 1-inch pieces. Soak mushrooms in hot water for 20 minutes. Discard the water and squeeze the mushrooms dry. Cut off and discard mushroom stems, then cut each cap into ½-inch slices. Lay sliced fish and mushrooms on top of tofu. Chop green onions; mince ginger and garlic.

Heat a wok or large skillet over high heat until hot; add oil and heat until hot. Add green onions, ginger, garlic, and dried shrimp; stir-fry for about 20 seconds until fragrant. Add vegetable stock and white pepper; cook until mixture boils. Pour mixture into saucepan containing tofu and bring to a boil, then simmer for 18 minutes with a cover. Sprinkle the soybeans on top of the tofu mixture and simmer another 2 minutes. Serve directly from the pot.

Serves 3 to 4.

TOFU SANDWICH
鍋貼豆腐

My mother served tofu dishes for breakfast, lunch, or dinner at least three to four times a week when we lived in Tainan, Taiwan. Tofu has always been quite reasonably priced, and it is nutritious, so it has become a staple food in most Chinese families. You do have to handle the tofu gently when you prepare this dish, as it is very easily torn.

INGREDIENTS
1 tub (16 ounces) firm tofu
¼ pound ground beef
½ teaspoon salt
1 teaspoon cornstarch
2 teaspoons rice wine
1 tablespoon water
¼ cup flour
2 to 3 tablespoons oil
2 teaspoons ginger, minced
2 teaspoons cornstarch and 2 teaspoons
   water to make a paste
1 tablespoon sesame oil
2 whole green onions, shredded

SEASONING SAUCE
1 cup beef stock
1 teaspoon sugar
1 tablespoon soy sauce
1 tablespoon oyster sauce

In a small mixing bowl, add salt, cornstarch, and wine to the ground beef. Add the water slowly to the meat mixture and stir with chopsticks or a fork until smooth. Divide the meat into 8 portions and set aside. In a small bowl, combine seasoning sauce.

Drain the tofu and slice it lengthwise into 16 pieces about ¼ inch thick. Lightly dust each tofu slice on both sides with flour. Spread the meat mixture evenly and smoothly over 8 pieces of tofu, then use the other 8 pieces to cover the meat mixture, making 8 tofu sandwiches.

Heat a flat frying pan over medium-low heat until hot; add oil and heat until hot. Pan-fry tofu sandwiches on each side until slightly brown (about 4 minutes). Remove the tofu sandwiches gently to a plate and keep warm.

Mince ginger and stir-fry with the remaining oil for 30 seconds. Add seasoning sauce and tofu sandwiches, then cover and let simmer for 3 to 4 minutes. Remove cover and stir in the cornstarch paste until tofu sandwiches are coated with seasoning sauce. Sprinkle with sesame oil. Garnish with shredded green onions.

Serves 2 to 3.

TOFU SHEET ROLLS WITH GLUTINOUS RICE
豆腐衣糯米卷

Another dish that is very Chinese is tofu sheet rolls combined with glutinous rice. To enhance the flavor of this dish, add a few links of Chinese sausage to the pot of rice while it's cooking. Once the rice is done, remove the sausages and dice them, then add to the rice and vegetable mixture.

INGREDIENTS

3 large pieces frozen tofu sheets
1 cup glutinous rice (sweet rice)
2 stalks celery, diced
1 small carrot, diced
2 whole green onions, chopped
4 large dried Chinese mushrooms, diced
2 teaspoons garlic, minced
3 to 4 tablespoons oil
2 tablespoons cornstarch mixed with 2
   tablespoons water to make a paste

SEASONING SAUCE

2 tablespoons oyster sauce
1 tablespoon hoisin sauce
½ teaspoon white pepper
2 teaspoons sesame oil

Wash rice well and soak in 2 cups of water for at least 2 hours. Drain well. Put rice in a pot and add 1¼ cups water. Cover and bring to a boil on medium heat. Stir once. Reduce heat to simmer and cook about 25 minutes.

In a small bowl, combine seasoning sauce. Dice celery and carrot; chop green onions. Soak mushrooms in hot water for 20 minutes. Discard the water and squeeze the mushrooms dry. Cut off and discard mushroom stems, then cut each cap into ¼-inch dice. Mince garlic.

Heat a wok or large skillet over medium-high heat until hot; add 1 tablespoon of oil and heat until hot. Stir-fry the garlic for 5 seconds. Add celery, carrot, green onions, and mushrooms and stir-fry for 1 minute. Add seasoning sauce and mix well with the vegetables. Remove from heat, add the rice, and mix thoroughly.

Bring frozen tofu sheets to room temperature and cut each sheet into 12 7-inch squares. Put 2 heaping tablespoons of rice-and-vegetable filling in one corner of a tofu sheet. With your hands, begin to roll into a cylinder about 4 to 5 inches long. Bring the two end flaps up over the top of the enclosed filling and press gently. Then continue to roll to the far point to form a neat roll. Moisten the tip with cornstarch paste and close the flap. Repeat until all the tofu rolls are made.

Heat a flat frying pan over medium-low heat until hot; add oil and heat until hot. Pan-fry rolls on each side until brown (about 3 minutes). Add more oil as needed. You can serve tofu rolls with Chinese dipping sauces (see page 126) or just eat them plain.

Makes 12 rolls.

TOFU SHEET ROLLS WITH SPICY SAUCE
麻辣豆魚

Tofu sheets (fu yi, 腐衣) are available only in Chinese stores. In fact, when I show this product to my students, they are amazed that there is no English writing on the package. This dish is simple to prepare and is great for vegetarians. If you are not a vegetarian, you can easily add any cooked meat along with the bean sprouts, celery, and carrots.

INGREDIENTS
1 large piece frozen tofu sheet
2 cups carrots, shredded
2 cups celery, shredded
2 cups bean sprouts
1 teaspoon salt
4 tablespoons oil
¼ cup green onion, minced
2 tablespoons toasted sesame seeds

SEASONING SAUCE
2 tablespoons sesame paste
3 tablespoons soy sauce plus 1 tablespoon water
1 tablespoon sugar
2 tablespoons sesame oil
2 teaspoons rice vinegar
1 teaspoon toasted Sichuan peppercorn powder (see page 169)
2 teaspoons chili oil

Bring the frozen tofu sheet to room temperature and keep it moist. Shred carrots and celery. In a large pot, bring 10 cups water to a boil and add 1 teaspoon salt. Parboil bean sprouts, carrots, and celery in the boiling water for 10 to 15 seconds. Remove and drain, then plunge vegetable mixture into ice water and drain again.

Cut the tofu sheet into 16 wedge-shaped pieces. Put about 1 heaping tablespoon of vegetable mixture on the wide end of a wedge. Beginning at the wide end, roll each piece into a tight roll. Place finished rolls on a plate. In a small bowl, combine seasoning sauce.

Heat a 9-inch skillet over medium-low heat until hot; add oil and heat until hot. Add tofu sheet rolls without allowing them to overlap. Fry each side until brown (about 4 to 5 minutes on each side). Remove to a plate and pour seasoning sauce over the rolls. Sprinkle green onion and sesame seeds on top.

Serves 3 to 4.

Vegetables

BUDDHA'S DELIGHT
羅漢齋

Even if you are not a vegetarian, you will love this dish. You can select any vegetables in season to prepare this dish. I use just 8 vegetables, but in some regions of China this dish includes as many as 18. This dish will definitely taste better when made with fresh ingredients. Be sure to parboil all your vegetables.

INGREDIENTS

4 ounces snow peas
4 ounces broccoli
1 large carrot or 1 cup baby carrots
½ can straw mushrooms (15-ounce can)
1 small kohlrabi, sliced
½ cup bamboo shoots, sliced
½ cup water chestnuts, sliced
6 ounces baby cabbage
½ can whole young corn (15-ounce can)
1 tablespoon ginger, minced
1 tablespoon garlic, minced
6 tablespoons oil
1 tablespoon cornstarch and 1 tablespoon
  water to make a paste

SEASONING SAUCE

2 tablespoons soy sauce
2 tablespoons vegetarian mushroom sauce
½ teaspoon salt
1 teaspoon sugar
1 tablespoon rice wine
½ tablespoon vinegar
¼ teaspoon white pepper
1 tablespoon sesame oil or chili oil
½ cup vegetable stock

String the snow peas. Cut broccoli into bite-sized pieces. Peel carrot. Slice carrots, straw mushrooms, kohlrabi, bamboo shoots, and water chestnuts. Drain canned corn (or other canned vegetables). Parboil all vegetables for 30 seconds, then drain. Mince ginger and garlic. In a small bowl, combine seasoning sauce.

Heat a wok or large skillet over high heat until hot; add oil and heat until hot. Add ginger and garlic and stir-fry briskly for 5 seconds. Add all parboiled vegetables, stir-fry for 1 minute, then add seasoning sauce. When the mixture boils, cover and cook vigorously for 2 minutes. Uncover and slowly stir in cornstarch paste until mixture thickens.

Serves 6 to 7.

CABBAGE ROLLS WITH CREAM SAUCE
奶油菜卷

Cabbage rolls are loved by people all over the world. This is a Cantonese dish which was influenced by Westerners, who introduced the use of butter and cream. If you are fond of cabbage, you will love this dish. You can make the rolls ahead of time and keep them in the freezer.

INGREDIENTS

1 medium green cabbage
½ teaspoon white pepper

FILLING

8 ounces shrimp
½ pound boneless and skinless chicken breasts
4 dried Chinese mushrooms, diced
4 ounces cooked ham, diced
1 cup bamboo shoots or water chestnuts, diced
5 tablespoons oil
4 tablespoons soy beans
½ teaspoon salt
½ cup chicken stock
1 tablespoon cornstarch and 1 tablespoon water to make a paste

MARINADE FOR SHRIMP

1 teaspoon rice wine
1 teaspoon cornstarch

MARINADE FOR CHICKEN

2 teaspoons soy sauce
2 teaspoons cornstarch

CREAM SAUCE

4 tablespoons butter
3 cups chicken stock (see page 18)
1 teaspoon salt
6 tablespoons cornstarch and 6 tablespoons water to make a paste
⅔ cup cream

In a bowl, mix shrimp marinade. Wash shrimp if desired. Shell shrimp and remove the black vein. Dry with paper towels and cut into ¼-inch dice. Marinate for 20 to 30 minutes. In another bowl, mix chicken marinade. Cut chicken breast into ¼-inch dice and marinate for 20 to 30 minutes. Soak mushrooms in hot water for 20 minutes. Discard the water and squeeze the mushrooms dry. Cut off and discard mushroom stems, then cut each cap into ¼-inch dice. Cut ham and bamboo shoots or water chestnuts into ¼-inch dice. Remove the core of the cabbage. Place cabbage in deep pot or wok of boiling water and gently remove softened leaves.

Heat a wok or large skillet over high heat until hot; add oil and heat until hot. Add shrimp and chicken and stir-fry briskly for 2 to 3 minutes until it becomes firm, then add mushrooms, ham, bamboo shoots or water chestnuts, and soybeans. Stir-fry for a few seconds, then add ½ teaspoon salt, ½ cup chicken stock, and cornstarch paste. Stir until glazed. Remove from wok. Place 2 to 3 tablespoons of filling in center of cabbage leaf and roll up like an egg roll. Seal with toothpick. Place cabbage rolls in a steamer and steam for 20 minutes.

Prepare cream sauce by heating butter and chicken stock until mixture boils. Add salt. Slowly stir in cornstarch paste until the mixture thickens. Add cream. Remove the steamed cabbage rolls to a platter and pour cream sauce over them. Sprinkle with white pepper.

Makes about 10 large or 12 medium-sized cabbage rolls.

DRY-COOKED GREEN BEANS
乾燒四季豆

Chinese green beans are much longer than Western green beans. The next time you visit an Asian market, buy some Chinese green beans to prepare this famous Sichuan dish. The deep-fried method is a must for this dish, but mind the extra calories! You can stir-fry instead, but the result is not as tasty. The leftover oil from deep-frying can be reused for general cooking. I always use a coffee filter to remove impurities from the oil before storing the oil in the refrigerator.

INGREDIENTS
4 ounces ground pork
1½ pounds green beans
1 tablespoon dried shrimp
½ cup Sichuan preserved mustard stems, minced
2 tablespoons green onion, chopped
2 teaspoons ginger, minced
2 cups oil
1 tablespoon rice vinegar
1 tablespoon sesame oil

SEASONING SAUCE
2 tablespoons soy sauce
1 tablespoon water
2 tablespoons rice wine
1 tablespoon sugar
½ teaspoon salt

Wash the green beans and pat dry with paper towels; snip off the ends. Cut into 2-inch lengths and place in a bowl. Soak dried shrimp in warm water for 20 minutes, drain, and mince fine. Rinse Sichuan preserved mustard stems briefly, then mince fine. Chop green onion and mince ginger. In a small bowl, combine seasoning sauce.

Heat 2 cups oil in a wok or large skillet until hot (about 375 degrees). Add one handful of green beans and deep-fry them until they are wrinkled and become soft. Remove them from the wok with a slotted spoon to a platter lined with a paper towel. Repeat until all green beans have been deep-fried.

Remove all but 2 tablespoons of oil from the wok, and heat the remainder another 5 seconds over high heat. Stir-fry the ginger for about 5 seconds. Add the ground pork, dried shrimp, and Sichuan preserved mustard stems and stir-fry briskly over high heat until the pork is cooked (about 1 minute). Add green beans and seasoning sauce; continue to cook over medium heat until almost all the liquid disappears. Add vinegar, sesame oil, and green onions to the beans and toss until the green onions are heated.

Serves 3 to 4.

EGGPLANT SICHUAN STYLE
魚香茄子

You can substitute regular eggplant to make this dish, but nowadays you can easily find Chinese eggplant at the supermarket. It is slightly sweet and almost seedless. This dish is very tasty if you like hot and spicy food. It can be served hot or cold.

INGREDIENTS

1¼ pounds Chinese eggplant
4 ounces ground pork
½ teaspoon salt
4 tablespoons oil
1 tablespoon ginger, minced
1 tablespoon garlic, minced
1 whole green onion, chopped
1 teaspoon dried red pepper powder
1 tablespoon hot bean sauce
1 tablespoon vinegar
1 tablespoon sesame oil

SEASONING SAUCE

1 tablespoon soy sauce
1 tablespoon rice wine
1 teaspoon sugar
¼ cup chicken stock

Preheat oven to 450 degrees. Rinse the eggplant and cut off the stems, then roll cut the eggplant. Put the cut eggplant in a bowl and add salt and 2 tablespoons of oil. Toss and mix well. Line a baking sheet with a silicone mat, add the eggplant, and bake in the hot oven for 15 minutes. You can also cook the eggplant in a covered wok over very low heat for 15 minutes. Mince ginger and garlic; chop green onion. In a small bowl, combine seasoning sauce.

Heat a wok or large skillet over high heat until hot; add 2 tablespoons of oil and heat until hot. Add ground pork and stir-fry well, then add ginger, garlic, red pepper powder, and hot bean sauce and stir for a few seconds. Add the seasoning sauce. Stir briefly, remove the eggplant from the oven, and add to the mixture. Stir constantly until the liquid starts to disappear. Add the green onion, vinegar, and sesame oil. Mix thoroughly and serve hot or cold.

Serves 3 to 4.

HOT CABBAGE PEKING STYLE
北京辣大白菜

In the United States, it is common to serve salad for lunch or dinner. In China, on the contrary, salad is almost exclusively served at banquets. I often use this dish as a first course when I entertain my friends. If you would like to add a little color to the salad, you can substitute 1½ pounds shredded green cabbage and ½ pound shredded carrot for 2 pounds napa cabbage. This dish will keep in the refrigerator for one week.

INGREDIENTS
2 pounds napa cabbage, shredded
1 tablespoon salt
2 to 4 dried red peppers, shredded
1 tablespoon ginger, shredded
5 tablespoons sesame oil
¼ teaspoon toasted Sichuan peppercorn powder (see page 169)
¼ cup vinegar
¼ cup sugar

Shred the cabbage crosswise; wash and pat dry with paper towels. Place in a large bowl, sprinkle with salt, mix well, and soak about 4 hours. Squeeze out water and put cabbage back in the bowl. Shred red peppers and ginger.

Heat a wok or small skillet on high heat until hot. Add sesame oil and toss in dried red peppers, pressing them into the oil until they turn dark. Add toasted Sichuan peppercorn powder and ginger and stir-fry for a few seconds. Add vinegar and sugar and bring to a boil. Pour the sauce over the cabbage and mix well. After the cabbage has been marinated for 4 hours, serve cold.

Serves 3 to 4.

LADY IN THE CABBAGE
美女菜心

If you are an artist, you may want to use ham strips and black sesame seeds to make the eyes, eyebrows, and mouth of a lady's face. This dish can be prepared one day ahead of time and steamed the next day. If you freeze it, just steam an extra 5 minutes when ready to serve. It will be very helpful if you use a food processor to mince the shrimp and bacon. If you can't find bok choy in your area, you can always substitute napa cabbage.

INGREDIENTS
14 small heads bok choy
2 cups chicken stock (see page 18)
2 teaspoons cornstarch
2 tablespoons soaked hair seaweed
¼ teaspoon salt
¼ teaspoon white pepper
2 teaspoons cornstarch and 2 teaspoons
    water to make a paste
2 teaspoons sesame oil
2 tablespoons cooked ham, minced

FILLING
1 pound shrimp, minced
2 strips bacon, minced
1 egg white, beaten
2 teaspoons cornstarch
1 teaspoon salt
1 tablespoon rice wine

Remove the leaves of each head of bok choy and save for other use. Cut stems into sections 4 to 5 inches long. Wash bok choy stems and pat dry with paper towels. Parboil the stems in chicken stock for 4 minutes. Drain and save the stock. Place the stems on the rim of a large platter. Arrange in a circle and sprinkle cornstarch on stems. Set aside.

Wash shrimp if desired. Shell shrimp and remove the black vein. Dry with paper towels. Mince the shrimp and bacon. Mix the filling thoroughly. Using an ice cream scoop, place about 2 tablespoons of the filling on the top end of each stem of bok choy, one stem at a time. The shrimp ball represents a lady's face. Arrange hair seaweed around each shrimp ball to look like a lady with long hair until you have decorated all 14 faces.

Steam the platter over high heat for 5 minutes. At the same time, prepare the sauce. Heat the chicken stock over medium heat. Add salt and white pepper. Slowly stir in cornstarch paste until chicken stock thickens. Add sesame oil. Remove the platter from the steamer. Pour off excess liquid if any, then pour the sauce over the cabbage. Sprinkle the minced ham in the center of the platter.

Serves 4 to 5.

SICHUAN CUCUMBER SALAD
麻辣黄瓜

If you are going to make this dish for a large group, drying the cucumbers with paper towels will be an onerous task. Try using a salad spinner or a large bath towel.

INGREDIENTS
3 medium cucumbers
2 teaspoons salt

SEASONING SAUCE
4 cloves garlic, minced
½ teaspoon toasted Sichuan peppercorn
  powder (see page 169)
1 teaspoon hot bean sauce
1 tablespoon vinegar
2 teaspoons sugar
2 tablespoons sesame oil
1 to 2 teaspoons chili oil

Clean cucumbers and cut in half lengthwise, then scoop out the seeds. Cut cucumber halves lengthwise into ½-inch strips. Then cut each strip crosswise into 2-inch pieces. Sprinkle with salt and set aside for 3 to 4 hours. Wash cucumbers in cold water; drain well, then dry well with paper towels. Place in a bowl. In a small bowl, combine seasoning sauce. Add seasoning sauce to cucumbers. Soak for about 4 hours. Serve cucumbers in the liquid.

Serves 3 to 4.

STUFFED TOMATOES
釀番茄

I find it very odd that some Americans love ketchup but won't eat raw or cooked tomatoes. I think this dish will open their eyes and change their minds. To easily peel tomato skins, use a knife to cut a 1½-inch crisscross into the bottom of the tomato before immersing the tomato in boiling water.

INGREDIENTS
8 medium firm ripe tomatoes
1 tablespoon cornstarch and 1 tablespoon
  water to make a paste
Chinese parsley, chopped

FILLING
½ pound ground pork
½ pound shrimp, chopped
6 water chestnuts, chopped

SEASONING SAUCE
3 tablespoons soy sauce
1 cup chicken stock
¼ teaspoon salt
2 teaspoons sugar

MARINADE
1 tablespoon soy sauce
2 tablespoons water
1 tablespoon rice wine
½ teaspoon salt
⅛ teaspoon white pepper

Bring a pot of water to a boil. Immerse the tomatoes in boiling water for 1 minute, then immediately in cold water, then drain and peel. Cut the tomatoes in half (not through the stem). Gently squeeze them to remove excess juice; dig out the seeds with your finger or small spoon. Invert the tomatoes on a rack to drain for 20 minutes while you prepare the stuffing.

In a bowl, mix marinade. Wash shrimp if desired. Shell shrimp and remove the black vein. Dry with paper towels and chop coarsely. Chop water chestnuts. Put the ground pork, shrimp, and water chestnuts in a medium-sized bowl. Add the marinade, mix well, and set aside for 10 minutes. This is the filling.

Divide the filling into 16 portions and mound into each tomato. Arrange the tomatoes, filling side up, in a heatproof dish. In a small bowl, combine seasoning sauce. Pour seasoning sauce over the tomatoes and steam for 15 minutes.

Drain and save the sauce from the stuffed tomatoes and keep the latter warm in the steamer. Bring the sauce to a low boil; turn heat low, add cornstarch paste to the sauce until it is smooth and thickened. Pour the sauce over the stuffed tomatoes and serve. Garnish with Chinese parsley.

Serves 4 to 5.

SWEET AND SOUR CUCUMBER SALAD
甜醋黄瓜

You can use one English cucumber instead of two regular cucumbers for this dish. Since English cucumbers hardly have any seeds, you don't need to scoop them out. I like to serve this salad with sliced, peeled mango on a bed of lettuce, with roasted pine nuts sprinkled on top.

INGREDIENTS
2 medium cucumbers
½ teaspoon salt
1½ tablespoons sesame oil
⅛ teaspoon toasted Sichuan peppercorn
    powder (see page 169)

SEASONING SAUCE
3 tablespoons sugar
3 tablespoons vinegar
½ teaspoon salt

Wash and peel cucumbers. Cut in half lengthwise and scoop out the seeds. Sprinkle with ½ teaspoon salt and set aside for 15 minutes. Slice each cucumber half into ⅛-inch-thick pieces and place in bowl. In a small bowl, combine seasoning sauce.

Heat a small pot over medium-high heat until hot; add sesame oil and stir-fry toasted Sichuan peppercorn powder for a few seconds. Add seasoning sauce. Cook until mixture boils, then pour over cucumbers. Soak for at least 3 hours before serving. Serve chilled.

Serves 2 to 3.

WINTER MELON STUFFED WITH HAM
火腿冬瓜夹

When I first came to this country in 1964, winter melon was hard to find in stores. Nowadays you can buy it in just about any Asian market. Winter melon usually is used only in making soup, but I would like to introduce this steamed dish to you. When you entertain your friends at home, you don't have to worry about last-minute stir-frying. The finished dish is both colorful and delicious.

INGREDIENTS
2 to 2½ pounds cut up winter melon
½ pound ground pork
6 ounces country ham
½ cup chicken stock
1 tablespoon cornstarch and 1 tablespoon
  water to make a paste
⅛ teaspoon white pepper
1 teaspoon sesame oil
Chinese parsley, chopped

MARINADE
1 tablespoon green onion, minced
1 teaspoon ginger, minced
½ teaspoon salt
1 teaspoon rice wine
2 teaspoons cornstarch
1 teaspoon sesame oil

Rinse and dry the melon with paper towels. Remove the pulp and seeds and peel off the skin. Cut the melon into 2 to 3 pieces about 2 inches wide, then cut them again crosswise into 1-inch sections. Make a slit in the center of each section about three-quarters of the way through. You should have about 15 to 18 pieces of melon.

In a bowl, mix marinade. Marinate the ground pork for 20 to 30 minutes. Cut the ham into thin slices, approximately the same size as the pieces of melon. Put 2 teaspoons of ground pork mixture into each melon slit, then insert a piece of ham into each slit along with the ground pork. The result looks like a melon sandwich. You can prepare this step a day in advance. Cover and refrigerate.

Put the melon sandwiches, meat side up, in a shallow heatproof bowl or pie pan. Pour the chicken stock over the melon sandwiches. Steam over high heat for 25 minutes. Remove the bowl or pie pan and pour off the juice into a glass measuring cup. You should have more than 1 cup of the hot, steaming juice. Let the juice cool off. Pour 1 cup of juice into a small saucepan. Turn heat to low and cook to a low boil. Slowly stir in cornstarch paste until the sauce thickens. Add white pepper and sesame oil to the sauce and pour over the melon sandwiches. Garnish with Chinese parsley.

Serves 4 to 5.

Rice and Noodles

CHICKEN LO MEIN
雞絲撈麵

Lo mein, which means stir-fried noodles in Cantonese, is a scrumptious snack and one of the most popular dim sum dishes. I love to prepare it for all kinds of occasions, such as potluck dinners and buffets, and to welcome new neighbors. You can substitute pork, beef, or turkey for chicken. This is a great dish for freezing and serving later.

INGREDIENTS

1 pound boneless and skinless chicken breasts
3 to 4 cups vegetables (celery, carrots, bean sprouts and/or leafy vegetables), shredded
2 whole green onions, shredded
1 pound spaghetti noodles or fresh egg noodles
1 tablespoon garlic, minced
8 tablespoons oil
½ cup soy sauce

MARINADE

1 tablespoon soy sauce
1 tablespoon rice wine
½ tablespoon cornstarch

In a bowl, mix marinade. Cut the chicken with the grain into 2-inch-wide strips. Then cut crosswise against the grain into ⅛-inch slices and marinate for 20 to 30 minutes. Shred the vegetables and set aside. Split the green onions lengthwise and cut into 2-inch-long sections. Cook noodles following instructions on package. Drain and rinse with hot water, then drain again. Mince garlic.

Heat a wok or large skillet over high heat until hot; add 4 tablespoons of oil and heat until hot. Stir-fry garlic for a few seconds. Add noodles and mix and toss thoroughly over medium heat with ¼ cup soy sauce for 2 to 3 minutes. Dish out onto a warm platter and keep warm. Clean and reheat the wok and add another 4 tablespoons of oil. Stir-fry green onion and chicken over high heat until the chicken pieces are white and firm (about 2 to 3 minutes). Add the vegetables. Stir and mix with chicken. Sprinkle ¼ cup soy sauce onto chicken and vegetables mixture. Mix well.

Either toss chicken/vegetables together with noodles in one serving dish; or place chicken/vegetables and noodles in separate containers, and when ready to serve, place portion of chicken/vegetables mix on top of noodles on individual plates.

Serves 4 to 5.

CHINESE BOILED RICE
白飯

I was the youngest of five children in the Lin family. Being the baby, I was pretty spoiled and didn't have to do any housework or cooking. I remember vividly that my mother only asked me to wash the rice until the water ran clear. My mother even taught me how to cook rice using the finger method to measure how much water to add to make perfect boiled rice. Over the years, I decided to use a measuring cup, which is a more reliable.

Nowadays I tend to buy rice that doesn't need to be washed. If you're not sure whether the rice needs to be washed, read the instructions on the package. If you have room in your kitchen, you may want to invest in a rice cooker. Not only will a rice cooker prepare the rice perfectly every time, you can program when you want the rice to be ready, and the machine will keep the rice warm and tasty for several hours.

INGREDIENTS
1 cup medium-grain rice and 1¼ cups cold water
- or -
1 cup long-grain rice and $1^{1}/_{3}$ cups cold water

Wash rice if desired. Put rice in a pot and add water. Cover. Bring to a boil on medium heat. Stir once. Reduce heat to simmer and cook about 20 to 25 minutes. Remove cover and fluff the rice with chopsticks or a fork.

Serves 3 to 4.

COLD SPICY NOODLES
涼拌麵

This dish is a salad and is great for potluck get-togethers. For the last 25 years, when I have taken it to various places, people have always asked me for the recipe. I love to prepare this one-dish meal because I can make it a day ahead of time and toss it just before serving. To make a meatless salad, omit the chicken and increase the noodles to 1 pound. You can also substitute cooked pork, beef, duck, or ham for chicken.

INGREDIENTS
12 ounces fresh egg noodles or spaghetti noodles
1 pound chicken breasts with bones
2 tablespoons sesame oil
1 cup bean sprouts
1 tablespoon rice wine
1 slice ginger, smashed
1 whole green onion, smashed
1 large cucumber, shredded
1 cup carrot, shredded
2 to 3 tablespoons chopped, roasted peanuts

SEASONING SAUCE
7 tablespoons soy sauce
3 tablespoons sesame paste
2 tablespoons rice vinegar
2 teaspoons sugar
1 tablespoon chili oil
3 tablespoons green onion, minced
½ tablespoon ginger, minced
½ tablespoon garlic, minced
2 tablespoons sesame oil
½ teaspoon toasted Sichuan peppercorn powder (see page 169)

Cook fresh noodles in 10 cups of boiling water for 5 minutes, then drain. (If spaghetti noodles are used, follow directions on the package.) Sprinkle with 2 tablespoons sesame oil and mix well. Set aside to cool. Boil bean sprouts in boiling water for 30 seconds; remove and drain. Soak in ice water.

Place chicken breasts in a deep pot of cold water and cook over high heat until water boils. Add rice wine, ginger, and green onion. Turn heat to medium-low and cook 15 to 20 minutes. Remove and drain. After the chicken cools off, remove the bones and shred the chicken into thin strips. Shred cucumber and carrot in separate bowls. In a small bowl, combine seasoning sauce.

Spread noodles over a large plate. Place shredded chicken on top of the noodles in the middle of the plate, then surround with carrots on either side, followed by bean sprouts and cucumbers. Refrigerate 3 to 4 hours. Pour seasoning sauce over the dish and sprinkle the roasted peanuts just before serving. Serve cold.

Variation
Substitute ½ pound of boneless chicken breasts for 1 pound of chicken breasts with bones. Preheat oven to 250 degrees. Place boneless chicken breasts on a cookie sheet and bake for 30 minutes. Shred the chicken into thin strips as described above.

Serves 5 to 8.

CURRIED RICE
咖喱飯

Chinese people have eaten boiled rice for thousands of years. My mother served us boiled rice for lunch and dinner every day. Once in a while we would have fried rice on the table for special occasions. Since my husband is a Caucasian, I always try to fix rice in ways other than boiled when served with not-so-highly-seasoned dishes. I created this curried rice dish myself, and it turns out to be quite popular with my family, guests, and students. In fact, my son Christopher told me that he likes curried rice better than fried rice.

INGREDIENTS
1 cup medium-grain rice or long-grain rice
1 teaspoon fresh garlic, minced
1 whole green onion, minced
2 tablespoons oil
1 teaspoon curry powder
½ teaspoon salt
1¼ cups water or chicken stock (see page 18) for medium-grain rice
or 1⅓ cups for long-grain rice

Mince garlic and onion. Heat a medium saucepan over high heat until hot; add oil and heat until hot. Stir-fry garlic and curry powder for 10 seconds. Add rice, salt, and water or chicken stock. Bring the mixture to a boil and stir once, then simmer for 20 to 25 minutes with a cover. Just before serving, fold the green onion into the hot rice.

Serves 3 to 4.

EMERALD FRIED RICE
翡翠炒飯

This fried rice is actually very similar to ham and egg fried rice. However, the essential ingredient in this fried rice is spinach or bok-choy cabbage. Once the rice is cooked with the spinach or cabbage leaves, it turns into a jade green color, which is quite attractive.

INGREDIENTS

12 ounces spinach
   or 1 pound bok-choy cabbage
2 teaspoons salt
4 Chinese sausages, diced
3 eggs, well beaten with dash of salt
1 teaspoon garlic, minced
7 tablespoons oil
4 cups cooked rice (see page 113)

Wash the spinach well and mince the leaves in batches in a food processor. If using bok-choy cabbage, remove the stems. Mix the minced spinach or cabbage with 1 teaspoon salt and set aside for 15 minutes. Squeeze dry using your hands or a towel. Steam the Chinese sausages for 20 minutes and dice into ¼-inch pieces. Beat eggs and mince garlic.

Heat a wok or large skillet over medium-high heat until hot; add 1 tablespoon of oil and heat until hot. Pour in the beaten eggs and make a small omelet. Remove the omelet and cut it into ¼-inch pieces.

Heat 6 tablespoons of oil in the same wok and add spinach, sausages, diced eggs, garlic, 1 teaspoon of salt, and cooked rice. Stir constantly for 2 to 3 minutes until the ingredients are well blended and heated.

Serves 5 to 6.

FRIED RICE REBEKAH'S WAY
和寧式炒飯

Over the years, when I cooked fried rice the traditional way at home or in my cooking classes, I often thought about making the process easier and quicker. Since I use a simple method to cook curried rice, why not cook fried rice the same way? The best part about serving fried rice is that you can cook it ahead of time and reheat it in the microwave. Many times I even freeze fried rice, then reheat in the microwave just before serving.

INGREDIENTS
2 cups long-grain rice
1 teaspoon garlic, minced
6 tablespoons oil
$2^2/_3$ cups water
1 teaspoon salt
2 tablespoons soy sauce
4 Chinese sausages, diced
1 pound frozen mixed vegetables, defrosted

Mince garlic. Heat a medium saucepan over medium-high heat until hot; add oil and heat until hot. Stir-fry garlic for 10 seconds. Add rice and water. Bring the mixture to a boil and add salt and soy sauce. Simmer for 25 minutes with a cover. Cut sausages into ¼-inch dice.

Five minutes before the rice is cooked, put the sausages and defrosted mixed vegetables into the saucepan and steam with the rice. When the rice is cooked, stir and toss until fluffy, light, and nicely blended.

Serves 5 to 6.

HAM AND EGG FRIED RICE
火腿蛋炒飯

This is the Cantonese way to cook this dish. When I was growing up in Taiwan, fried rice was never served at a regular meal, since it was considered a snack. When I traveled by train between my home and the university in Taipei, fried rice was often served in the dining coaches. I always looked forward to the fluffy and delicious Ham and Egg Fried Rice. Although people in other regions of China also consume fried rice, soy sauce usually is not used in its preparation. Fried rice is great as a leftover; you can freeze it and reheat in the microwave.

INGREDIENTS
4 cups cooked rice (see page 113)
3 eggs, well beaten with dash of salt
3 whole green onions, minced or chopped
1 cup ham, diced
1 teaspoon garlic, minced
1 cup defrosted frozen soybeans, chopped
6 tablespoons oil
2 tablespoons soy sauce
1 teaspoon salt

Beat eggs, mince or chop green onions, and cut ham into ¼-inch dice. Mince garlic and chop soybeans. Heat a wok or large skillet over high heat until hot; add oil and heat until hot. Pour in the beaten eggs and stir-fry quickly until eggs are in tiny pieces. Add rice, green onions, ham, garlic, soybeans, soy sauce, and salt. Stir constantly for 2 to 3 minutes until the ingredients are well blended and heated.

Variation
Substitute other cooked meat or shellfish for ham in the same quantity as above. Cooked pork, beef, shrimp, chicken, or Chinese roast pork are all good.

Serves 5 to 6.

LOTUS LEAF RICE WRAPS
荷葉包米

The Chinese won't throw away any useable part of this water plant. Lotus roots are used in soups or braised dishes and lotus seeds in desserts and snacks. Lotus leaves are also sold in most Asian supermarkets and are ideal wrapping for steamed rice, fish, meat, and poultry dishes. They give a delicately fragrant and moist texture to the food. This dish can be made with cooked short-grain rice instead of cooked glutinous rice.

INGREDIENTS
5 dried lotus leaves
5 cups cooked glutinous rice (see page 128)
14 20-inch lengths of twine

FILLING
½ pound pork, diced
½ pound shrimp, diced
6 dried Chinese mushrooms, diced
3 Chinese sausages, diced
1 small shallot, chopped
1 tablespoon ginger, minced
4 tablespoons oil

SEASONING SAUCE
2 tablespoons soy sauce
2 tablespoons oyster sauce
2 tablespoons rice wine
1 tablespoon cornstarch with 1 tablespoon
  water to make a paste

MARINADE
1 tablespoon soy sauce
½ tablespoon cornstarch
1 tablespoon rice wine

Soak lotus leaves in hot water until softened (about 30 minutes). Drain. Open a leaf (almost 2 feet in diameter) and cut out the pointed center peak with scissors. Cut out 3 8-inch-round pieces from each leaf. Cut the rest of the lotus leaves the same way until you get 15 round pieces. Set them aside and keep moist.

Cut pork with the grain into ¼-inch slices. Then cut again with the grain into ¼-inch strips. Put the strips together and cut across the grain into ¼-inch dice. Wash shrimp if desired. Shell shrimp and remove the black vein. Dry with paper towels and cut into ¼-inch dice. In a bowl, mix marinade. Marinate pork and shrimp for 20 to 30 minutes. Soak mushrooms in hot water for 20 minutes. Discard the water and squeeze the mushrooms dry. Cut off and discard mushroom stems, then cut each cap into ¼-inch dice. Cut Chinese sausages into ¼-inch dice. Chop shallot and mince ginger. In a small bowl, combine seasoning sauce.

Heat a wok or large skillet over medium-low heat until hot; add oil and heat until hot. Stir-fry the shallot until it becomes caramelized. Turn heat to high; add ginger and cook for 5 seconds. Add pork, shrimp, mushrooms, and sausages and stir-fry for 3 minutes. Add seasoning sauce and cook until sauce thickens. Remove from heat and allow to cool. This is the filling.

Place lotus leaves on work surface. Put heaping ¼ cup of rice into the center of each leaf. Place 2 tablespoons of filling over rice. Fold leaf over rice mixture to form a package and secure with twine. Steam for 15 minutes. Cut open to serve.

Makes 12 to 14.

SICHUAN RED-COOKED SPICY BEEF WITH NOODLES
四川牛肉麵

In the United States, birthday celebrations are significant events for young children. Growing up in China, I usually got a bowl of noodle soup and two hard-boiled eggs for my birthday. No presents, no celebrations. Noodles symbolize long life, and two eggs represent two zeros, meaning you are supposed to live 100 years. When making the seasoning sauce for this dish, I use a tea ball filled with Sichuan peppercorns and star anise to enhance the soup flavor.

INGREDIENTS
2 pounds bottom round roast
1 cup sour mustard greens, chopped
1 pound napa cabbage or spinach
2 whole green onions, smashed
4 slices ginger, smashed
4 large cloves garlic, smashed
4 tablespoons oil
1 tablespoon hot bean sauce
1 pound fresh noodles

SEASONING SAUCE
6 cups water
¼ cup dark soy sauce
1 teaspoon Sichuan peppercorns
2 whole star anise
¼ cup rice wine
½ teaspoon salt
1 tablespoon sugar
2 to 3 pieces dried red peppers

INDIVIDUAL SEASONING SAUCE
1 teaspoon sesame oil
2 teaspoons Chinese parsley, chopped
Dash of black pepper
1 tablespoon green onion, minced
½ teaspoon chili oil, chili sauce, or chili
   paste with garlic

Cut the meat lengthwise into 1½-inch-wide strips, then cut the strips crosswise into 1½-inch cubes. In a large bowl, combine seasoning sauce. Chop the sour mustard greens and cut the cabbage or spinach into 1½-inch sections. If you use cabbage, separate the stems. Smash green onions, ginger, and garlic.

Heat a wok or large skillet over medium-high heat until hot; add 4 tablespoons of oil and heat until hot. Stir-fry sour mustard greens, green onion, ginger, garlic, and hot bean sauce for 1 minute. Turn heat to high and add meat; stir and flip until the meat is seared on all sides (about 1 to 3 minutes). Add seasoning sauce. Turn heat to low, cover, and simmer for 2 hours until the meat is tender. Boil the noodles according to the directions on the package. Cook cabbage in spicy beef mixture, 4 minutes for stems and 1 minute for leaves, or 1 minute for spinach.

Combine individual seasoning sauce and pour into individual bowls. Add desired amount of noodles and cabbage or spinach. Finally, add red-cooked spicy beef.

Serves 4 to 6 as a snack.

STIR-FRIED RICE NOODLES WITH MEAT
炒米粉

This is a southern noodles dish made from ground rice. Actually, there are two kinds of rice noodles in southern China: thin rice noodles and Cantonese style ho fen. To buy fresh rice noodles is a little difficult nowadays, but there are plenty of dried rice noodles that can be bought in all Asian supermarkets. You must first soak them in hot water for 5 minutes or cold water for 15 to 20 minutes. Drain and discard the water, then cut the noodles in half with scissors. The noodles are ready to be used.

INGREDIENTS
1 pound rice noodles
1 pound pork or beef, shredded
8 dried Chinese mushrooms, shredded
1 pound napa cabbage, shredded
1 tablespoon ginger, minced
1 tablespoon garlic, minced
8 tablespoons oil
½ teaspoon salt

SEASONING SAUCE
¼ cup soy sauce
2 tablespoons rice wine
½ teaspoon sugar
½ teaspoon salt
⅛ teaspoon white pepper
1 cup chicken stock

MARINADE
1 tablespoon rice wine
1 tablespoon soy sauce
1 teaspoon cornstarch

In a bowl, mix marinade. In a large bowl, cover the rice noodles with hot water for 5 minutes, then drain thoroughly in a colander. Cut the pork or beef against the grain into ⅛-inch-thick slices. Then cut the slices into 1½- to 2-inch-long shreds. Marinate for 20 to 30 minutes. Soak mushrooms in hot water for 20 minutes. Discard the water and squeeze the mushrooms dry. Cut off and discard mushroom stems, then cut each cap into ¼-inch strips. Cut cabbage into 2-inch-long and ⅛-inch-wide shreds. Mince ginger and garlic. In a small bowl, combine seasoning sauce.

Heat a wok or large skillet over high heat until hot; add 4 tablespoons of oil and heat until hot. Add rice noodles and salt, and cook for 2 minutes. Remove to a plate or a bowl.

Heat a wok or large skillet over high heat until hot; add 3 to 4 tablespoons of oil and heat until hot. Stir-fry ginger and garlic for 10 seconds. Add meat and stir-fry for 2 minutes. Add mushrooms and cabbage to the meat mixture and cook for 1 to 2 minutes. Add rice noodles and seasoning sauce, stirring mixture until the liquid is completely absorbed.

Serves 9 to 10.

Dim Sum

Basic Yeast Dough
發麵

Making this basic yeast dough is a laborious task. Even my mother, who was a great cook, made it only once in a while. My sisters and I weren't much help, since this dough requires a lot of muscle work (I have an older brother who always seemed to be away from home). When my mother visited me in 1981, she was amazed and shocked to watch me use a food processor to knead the dough. This dough will keep three days in the refrigerator. Grease top of dough and cover with plastic wrap. When ready to use, let stand at room temperature for 45 minutes to 1 hour, or until smooth and soft.

INGREDIENTS
7 cups all-purpose flour
2 packages dry yeast
6 tablespoons sugar
1 cup warm water (about 110 degrees F)
1 cup plus 2 tablespoons cold water
2 tablespoons oil
½ teaspoon salt
2 teaspoons baking powder

Dissolve the yeast and 2 tablespoons sugar in 1 cup warm water and let stand for 10 minutes, then add 1 cup plus 2 tablespoons cold water to the yeast mixture. Pour the flour into a large bowl and stir in the remaining sugar, oil, and salt. Make a well in the center and pour in the dissolved yeast mixture, mixing with your hands until all the ingredients are well combined and slightly firm dough is formed.

Place the dough on a lightly floured surface and knead it by pushing and turning with the heel of your hand for 5 to 8 minutes. Sprinkle the dough with flour from time to time if too sticky. Place the dough in a large greased bowl, cover the bowl with a lightly damped towel, and let it set in a warm place for 1½ to 2 hours, or until the dough doubles in bulk.

Turn the dough out on a lightly floured board, then sprinkle the baking powder over it. Knead vigorously for 5 minutes until the dough is smooth and elastic.

Note: A food processor or a heavy-duty electric mixer can be used to prepare the dough.

CHINESE BEEF JERKY
牛肉乾

Beef jerky is an ideal snack for traveling or camping, or just to eat for fun. In China, eating beef jerky in the movie theater is as popular as eating popcorn in the United States. You can easily buy ready-made beef jerky in an Asian market, but homemade beef jerky is definitely tastier.

INGREDIENTS

2 pounds beef bottom round
2 cups water
3 slices ginger, smashed
2 whole green onions, smashed
1 whole star anise
1 tablespoon dried orange peels
½ stick cinnamon
1 teaspoon fennel seeds, crushed
1 teaspoon coriander seeds, crushed

SEASONING SAUCE

1 tablespoon soy sauce
3 tablespoons sugar
1 teaspoon salt
4 tablespoons beef stock
1 tablespoon rice wine

Cut beef into eight ¼-pound pieces. Place a large, deep pot over high heat; add beef, water, ginger, green onions, star anise, orange peels, stick cinnamon, fennel seeds, and coriander seeds. After the water comes to a boil, turn heat to low and cook 1 to 2 hours until the meat is tender. Cut beef along the grain into ⅛-inch slices. In a small bowl, combine seasoning sauce.

Heat a wok or large skillet over high heat. Add beef slices and seasoning sauce and stir-fry until mixture is dry (about 8 to 10 minutes). Remove and spread slices flat on greased cookie sheets. Bake in preheated oven at 200 degrees. Bake one side for 45 minutes, then turn over and bake other side another 45 minutes. After the beef slices have cooled, store them in an airtight container.

Variations

Spicy hot dried beef: Add ½ to 1 teaspoon red pepper powder to seasoning sauce.
Curry dried beef: Add 1 tablespoon curry powder to seasoning sauce.
Curry and spicy hot dried beef: Add 1 tablespoon curry powder and ½ teaspoon red pepper powder to seasoning sauce.

Makes about 1 pound dried beef.

CHINESE DIPPING SAUCES
沾醬

Some dim sum dishes, such as Pot Stickers, Shao Mai, Spring Rolls, Fried Wontons and Har Gow, taste extra good when eaten with sauces. These sauces are easily made and can be stored in the freezer. Sweet and sour sauce is like an ice cream that will never become hard. It can be removed from its container with a scoop and reheated in the microwave or on the stovetop. The other sauces below can easily be made at the last minute before serving.

SWEET AND SOUR SAUCE 甜酸醬

INGREDIENTS
½ cup sugar
½ teaspoon salt
3 tablespoons ketchup
½ cup vinegar
3 tablespoons cornstarch
1 cup water

Cook sugar, salt, ketchup, and vinegar over medium-high heat until the sauce has the consistency of syrup. Mix the cornstarch and water. Add this to the sauce and cook until thick. Keep warm. Makes about 1½ cups of sauce.

SOY AND VINEGAR SAUCE 醬油和醋

The combination of soy sauce and vinegar is as popular in China as ketchup is in America. When you make this sauce, you can add varieties of spicy ingredients to the mixture. There are many spicy condiments in Asian markets to choose from. In my cooking class, I usually recommend chili oil, chili paste with garlic, ground fresh chili paste, and hot pepper sauce.

INGREDIENTS
¼ cup soy sauce
¼ cup or less of rice vinegar
2 tablespoons green onion, minced
1 tablespoon sesame oil
1 teaspoon ginger, minced
1 teaspoon garlic, minced

In a small bowl, combine all ingredients until evenly blended.

MUSTARD SAUCE 芥末醬

INGREDIENTS
1 to 2 tablespoons dry mustard powder
2 tablespoons rice wine
½ teaspoon sesame oil

In a small bowl, combine all ingredients until evenly blended.

CHINESE ONION PANCAKES
葱油餅

It's amazing that these pancakes are made with only a few ingredients, yet taste so wonderful. I usually make one pancake at a time. Brush one side of the pancake with a pastry brush dipped in oil, then pan-fry until slightly brown. While the bottom side of the pancake is cooking, brush the top side, then turn over and pan-fry so that both sides are now cooked.

INGREDIENTS
2 cups all-purpose flour
2 teaspoons salt
$^2/_3$ cup boiling water
6 to 8 tablespoons oil
$^1/_2$ to 1 cup green onion, chopped

Put the flour and salt into a large mixing bowl. Gradually add the boiling water, and with a pair of chopsticks stir to make a soft dough (add a little more water if dough is not soft enough). Knead it until it feels smooth. Put the dough back into the bowl and cover with a damp cloth. Let the dough stand for about 20 to 30 minutes.

Turn dough onto a lightly floured surface and knead again for 1 to 2 minutes. Divide the dough into 8 pieces. Use a rolling pin and roll each piece until it is round and flat (about $^1/_8$ inch thick). Coat each piece with a thin layer of oil. Sprinkle 1 to 2 tablespoons green onion evenly on the first piece of dough. Roll the dough into a jelly-like roll. Coil the roll into a patty, tucking the end of the roll underneath the patty. Gently press with your hand and roll flat with a rolling pin into a pancake about $^1/_4$ inch thick and 4 to 5 inches in diameter. Repeat procedure with the other 7 pieces of dough.

Heat a frying pan over medium heat. Add 2 teaspoons oil and fry pancakes one at a time until both sides are brown and crisp (about 5 minutes). Cut each pancake into 6 pieces.

Makes 8 pancakes.

CRISPY RICE
鍋巴

As I mention in my recipe for Shrimp Soup with Crispy Rice on page 23, you can buy crispy rice ready-made. Still, it's nice to know how to make it yourself in case you happen to be in a location where the product can't be found in stores. Crispy rice is also ideal for a snack, like potato chips or pretzels. If stored in an airtight container, crispy rice will keep in the freezer for months.

INGREDIENTS
1 pound glutinous rice (sweet rice)
¼ teaspoon salt

To prepare glutinous rice, wash rice well and soak in 2 cups of water for at least 2 hours. Drain well. Place rice in a steamer lined with a damp cloth. Steam for 45 minutes. Turn off the heat and let rice stand for another 15 minutes.

Add salt and mix the rice thoroughly. Put rice on a greased cookie sheet and flatten with a spatula until thin and smooth. Bake in preheated oven at 225 degrees for 2 hours. Some pieces around the edge of the cookie sheet will dry earlier than the rest, so remove them first by breaking into pieces. You also can dry the rice in sunlight.

CURRY PUFFS
咖喱餃

Chinese curry puffs are a challenge to make. When I was younger and first married, I would use only the authentic homemade dough. Over the years, I've developed so many hobbies that I've decided not to be a superwoman anymore. Once I discovered ready-made puff pastry sheets (see next recipe), I seldom reverted to making the pastry by hand.

DOUGH A
3 cups all-purpose flour
1 teaspoon salt
½ cup shortening
½ cup ice water

In a large mixing bowl combine the flour with salt and shortening. Work with your fingers until the shortening is evenly mixed in and has the grain of cornmeal. Stir in the ice water and mix and pat into a big ball. Set aside for 30 minutes.

DOUGH B
2½ cups all-purpose flour
²/₃ cup oil

In another mixing bowl, combine the flour with oil. Mix well and set aside for 30 minutes.

FILLING
1 pound ground beef
2 tablespoons oil
3 tablespoons soy sauce
1 teaspoon salt
1 teaspoon sugar
1 cup onion, minced
½ cup defrosted frozen soybeans, minced
2 to 3 tablespoons curry powder
3 egg yolks, well beaten

Heat a wok or large skillet over high heat until hot; add 1 tablespoon of oil and heat until hot. Stir-fry the beef until it separates into bits. Add soy sauce, salt, and sugar. Stir and mix well, then remove and set aside. Mince onion and soybeans. Heat the same wok with 1 tablespoon of oil. Stir-fry the onion until it wilts, then add the curry powder. Stir and cook the onion for another minute. Add the cooked meat and soybeans. Stir and mix thoroughly. Let cool, then put in the refrigerator to chill.

Roll Dough A into a circle about 6 inches in diameter. Set Dough B on top of the Dough A circle. Fold bottom side of Dough A halfway over Dough B. Fold right side of Dough A halfway over Dough B. Fold left side to overlap the right side. Then fold top side completely forward. Roll dough out to another 6-inch-diameter circle. Cut into 4 portions and set aside.

On a lightly floured surface, roll out one portion of dough at a time into a circle about ¹/₁₆-inch thick. Using a cookie-cutter, cut out circles about 3 inches in diameter. Knead the scraps into the remaining dough to make more circles.

Place about 2 heaping teaspoons of filling in the center of each round, fold over into a half-moon shape and seal the edges tightly, making a scalloped edge. Place the puffs on an ungreased baking sheet. Brush the tops with beaten egg yolks. Bake in a 400-degree oven for about 20 minutes.

Makes about 40 to 45 puffs.

CURRY PUFFS REBEKAH'S WAY
和寧咖喱餃

Chinese curry puffs were one of my favorite dim sum dishes when I was growing up in Taiwan. It is very time consuming and truly a labor of love to make this finger food from scratch. I discovered that using ready-made crust is a wonderful way to shorten the preparation of this scrumptious dish.

INGREDIENTS
3 packages (1.1 pounds each) puff pastry
   sheets
4 egg yolks, well beaten
Toasted sesame seeds

FILLING
1 pound ground beef
2 tablespoons oil
3 tablespoons soy sauce
½ teaspoon salt
1 teaspoon sugar
1 cup onion, minced
2 to 3 tablespoons curry powder
½ cup defrosted frozen soybeans, minced

Heat a wok or large skillet over high heat until hot; add 1 tablespoon of oil and heat until hot. Stir-fry the beef until it separates into bits. Add soy sauce, salt, and sugar. Stir and mix well, then remove and set aside. Mince onion and soybeans. Heat the same wok with 1 tablespoon of oil. Stir-fry the onion until it wilts, then add the curry powder. Stir and cook the onion for another minute. Add the cooked meat and soybeans. Stir and mix thoroughly. Let cool, then put in the refrigerator to chill.

Open 1 pastry sheet (9 inches x 10 inches). With a rolling pin, roll sheet to lengthen from 10 inches to 12 inches. Cut sheet into 12 3-inch x 3-inch pieces. Add 1 heaping tablespoon of filling in the center of each piece, fold piece in half to make a triangle, and seal the edge by pinching with your fingers.

Take the two ends in the fingers of both hands and bend them toward each other until the ends meet and overlap. Pinch the ends firmly together to seal. Repeat this process with the other pieces of pastry. Brush the top side of each puff with egg yolk, then sprinkle with toasted sesame seeds. Place the puffs on an ungreased baking sheet. Bake in a 400-degree oven for about 20 minutes.

Makes 72 puffs.

FLOWER ROLLS
花卷

For people living in northern China, flower rolls are quite popular. Long before I was born, my parents resided in Beijing for many years, and my mother often served these rolls with "red-cooked" dishes. Like bread served with western dishes, flower rolls are a very important part of the meal and often are used for soaking up juice or gravy. The Chinese have made this type of bread in the steamer for many centuries.

INGREDIENTS
1 recipe Basic Yeast Dough (see page 124)
4 tablespoons sesame oil

Divide the yeast dough into 4 parts. Roll each into a rectangular sheet about 12 inches long and 8 inches wide. Brush the top of each sheet with 1 tablespoon sesame oil. Tightly roll the sheets of dough lengthwise into jelly-like rolls, each about 1½ inches in diameter. Cut each roll crosswise with a sharp knife into twelve 1-inch pieces.

Press one piece on top of another firmly. Then press a chopstick crosswise hard down the middle of the top piece; the rolled ends of the top piece will lift up. (During the steaming process, these folds, and those on the bottom too, will separate to look like flower petals.) Repeat with the other pieces until all flower rolls are formed. Set them on a lightly floured tray or cookie sheet 1 to 2 inches apart under a dry towel. Let rise for about 45 minutes, until double in size.

Place buns, not touching, in a steamer lined with a damp cloth. Steam the buns over high heat for 12 minutes. Turn off the heat and wait a few seconds for the steam to subside before uncovering and removing the buns to a platter.

Variation
To dress these up a little, add 1 teaspoon of salt to the 4 tablespoons of sesame oil and brush the tops of the dough sheets as before. Then scatter 1 tablespoon of finely chopped green onions over each sheet and roll up into a tight jellyroll shape. Form the flower rolls and let them rise, then steam.

Makes 48 flower rolls.

FRIED WONTONS
炸餛飩

These are great for cocktail parties or as an appetizer. The best thing about this finger food is that it can be made ahead of time. Deep-fry the wontons until slightly brown and keep them in the refrigerator after they cool off, or you can make them weeks ahead and freeze them. Heat refrigerated wontons in an oven at 400 degrees for 15 to 20 minutes. If you use frozen wontons, heat at 425 degrees for 25 to 30 minutes.

INGREDIENTS
1 pound ground pork
1 egg, well beaten
2 tablespoons green onion, minced
1 tablespoon sesame oil
1 teaspoon salt
2 teaspoons cornstarch
1 tablespoon rice wine
2 tablespoons soy sauce
3 to 4 tablespoons water
Wonton wrappers

Mix all the above ingredients (except wrappers) in a large bowl, being sure to add the water 1 tablespoon at a time. Mix until smooth. Set aside until ready to use. This is the wonton filling. Put 1 teaspoon of filling in the center of each square of wonton skin and fold corner to corner to make a triangle. Take the two ends in the fingers of both hands and bend them toward each other until the ends meet and overlap. Pinch the ends firmly together with water to seal. Deep-fry wontons in oil at 375 degrees until golden. Serve with Chinese dipping sauces (see page 126).

Makes 70 to 80 fried wontons.

HAR GOW (SHRIMP DUMPLINGS)
蝦餃

These delicious, translucent shrimp dumplings are a very famous Cantonese dim sum dish. You can't buy the wrappers off the shelf, but they aren't that hard to make, even though they have to be prepared by hand (the dough is too soft to be kneaded in a food processor). A tortilla press makes the process easier. Apply a little oil to both sides of the press when making the wrappers.

DOUGH
3 cups sifted wheat starch
1 cup sifted tapioca flour
3 cups (approximately) boiling water
4 tablespoons oil

Combine the wheat starch and tapioca flour in a large mixing bowl. Gradually add the boiling water, stirring with chopsticks or a fork, then add the oil. Knead the dough until soft and satiny. Divide the dough into 4 portions. Place one portion on a lightly oiled surface and cover the other portions in a bowl. Knead the first portion of dough and roll into a long sausage shape about 1 inch in diameter. Cut crosswise into 1-inch pieces. Cover the dough with a slightly damp cloth to prevent it from drying.

Flatten one piece of dough with palm of hand into a ¼-inch-thick piece, then use a rolling pin to roll out each piece to form a circular wrapper 3 to 3½ inches in diameter. (It's easier to handle the dough if you use a little oil on your hands and rolling pin.) Do the same with all the pieces. The wrappers are now ready to be filled with shrimp mixture. Repeat above process with the other three portions of dough.

FILLING
1 pound shrimp, finely chopped
2 strips fatty bacon, minced
1 whole green onion, minced
4 tablespoons water chestnuts or bamboo
   shoots, finely chopped
1 egg white

2 teaspoons rice wine
2 teaspoons cornstarch
⅛ teaspoon white pepper
1 teaspoon salt
2 teaspoons sesame oil

Wash shrimp if desired. Shell shrimp and remove the black vein. Dry with paper towels and chop finely. Mince bacon and green onion. Finely chop water chestnuts or bamboo shoots. Place all filling ingredients in a bowl and stir in one direction, mixing thoroughly.

Place about 2 teaspoons of filling in the center of each wrapper. Fold the wrapper in half to cover the filling and form a half moon shape. Starting from the center, then the two sides, pinch the wrapper tightly together. Continue until you have used up the filling. Without crowding, place har gow in a steamer lined with a damp cloth or parchment paper. Cover and steam for 6 to 7 minutes.

Makes about 40 har gow.

LOTUS LEAF BUNS
荷葉夾

Lotus leaf buns are delicious to eat with Sichuan Duck. Wrap the duck meat inside the buns like a sandwich. This is a pure delight! Allow steamed lotus leaf buns to cool off, then store them in an airtight container or storage bag. They will keep for about ten days in the refrigerator or for weeks in the freezer. To reheat, steam frozen buns for 5 minutes. You can also wrap the buns in a damp paper towel and microwave for 1 minute if frozen or 20 seconds if refrigerated.

INGREDIENTS
1 recipe Basic Yeast Dough (see page 124)
Sesame oil or vegetable oil

Divide the dough into 4 equal portions. Roll the dough into a sausage-shaped roll about 1½ inches in diameter. Slice roll into 1-inch pieces. With the palm of the hand, flatten each piece into a circle, then roll with a small rolling pin into a pancake 3 to 4 inches in diameter. Brush lightly with sesame oil or vegetable oil and fold pancake in half. Using a sharp knife, score the top lengthwise like the vein of a leaf. Pinch in the flat side between thumb and forefinger to form a lotus leaf shape.

Place finished buns 1 inch apart in a steamer lined with a damp cloth or parchment paper. Let them set for a half hour, or until light. Repeat with the rest of the dough until all buns are made. Steam for 7 minutes.

Makes about 40 buns.

MANDARIN PANCAKES
薄餅

You can prepare these pancakes ahead of time and freeze them. Steam for 10 minutes when ready to serve.

INGREDIENTS
2 cups all purpose flour
¾ cup boiling water or a little less
1 tablespoon vegetable oil

Put flour in a large bowl and gradually pour in the boiling water while stirring with chopsticks or a fork. Let the dough cool, then knead the flour mixture until smooth. Cover with a damp cloth and let stand 20 minutes.

Cut the dough in half. Cover one half with a damp cloth for later use. Take the other half and roll into a long sausage shape. Cut into 12 pieces. Flatten each piece with palm of hand. Brush the tops of all pieces with oil. Place 6 pieces on top of the other six, oiled sides together. With a rolling pin, flatten into sandwiches 5 to 6 inches in diameter.

Preheat a griddle 320 degrees or a flat frying pan over medium-low heat. Fry each pancake until both sides turn brown. Remove and separate the two sides of each pancake while still hot.

Repeat the same method to finish the other half of dough. After pancakes have been cooked and separated, steam them for 5 minutes before serving.

Makes 24 Mandarin pancakes.

PHOENIX EYE DUMPLINGS
鳳眼餃

The Chinese like to name dishes after mythological creatures – such as the dragon, the phoenix, and the lion – because they symbolize their emperors and empresses. When these terms are used, the dishes usually are of high quality and great taste. I remember once telling my students that my mother was preparing Lion's Head for dinner. They asked me if this dish really was made from a lion's head! I replied that it was actually just a giant meatball.

INGREDIENTS
1 pound shrimp, minced
2 strips fatty bacon, minced
6 water chestnuts, minced
½ small carrot, minced
2 teaspoons ginger, minced
2 teaspoons garlic, minced
4 tablespoons ready-made fried red onion,
   already chopped or minced
1 package round dumpling wrappers

SEASONING
2 tablespoons rice wine
1 teaspoon salt
1 teaspoon sugar
1 teaspoon sesame oil
1 teaspoon cornstarch
¼ teaspoon white pepper

Wash shrimp if desired. Shell shrimp and remove the black vein. Dry with paper towels. With a cleaver, or using a food processor, mince the shrimp, bacon, water chestnuts, carrot, ginger, and garlic. In a medium bowl, combine the mixture from the food processor with the red onion and seasoning. Stir until thoroughly mixed. This is the filling.

Place a tablespoon of filling on a wrapper. Gather opposite edges and pinch together at the midpoint, using water to seal. Your wrapper should look like a taco sealed at the top. Take one outside edge and press against the sealed midpoint, creating two flaps. Wrap the flaps around a finger or chopstick to create the phoenix eye. Repeat process with the other outside edge. Arrange dumplings in a steamer lined with a damp cloth or parchment paper and steam for about 10 minutes. Serve with soy and vinegar sauce (see page 126).

Makes about 30 phoenix eye dumplings.

POT STICKERS
鍋貼

This is a northern snack which traditionally was served on the first morning of the Chinese New Year. Pot stickers are said to bring good luck all year round. My mother was really an expert in making this delectable dish. When I was in grade school, it was a family affair to make this snack; only my father was exempt from doing it. Since all of us were so fond of pot stickers, we made them quite often. I remember my father always said, "After you are full, you still have room for another ten!"

INGREDIENTS

1½ pounds ground pork (don't get lean pork; fat makes for juicy and flavorful pot stickers)
1½ pounds napa cabbage, chopped
¼ cup green onion, minced
1 tablespoon ginger, minced
1 tablespoon garlic, minced
2 teaspoons salt
2 tablespoons soy sauce

1 teaspoon sugar
4 teaspoons cornstarch
2 tablespoons water
3 tablespoons sesame oil
2 packages round dumpling wrappers or 1 recipe Pot Sticker Wrappers (see page 140)
2 to 3 tablespoons oil

Making the filling

Chop the cabbage by hand or using a food processor. Squeeze the excess liquid from the cabbage. Mince green onion, ginger, and garlic. Put the ground pork, green onion, ginger, garlic, salt, soy sauce, sugar, and cornstarch in a large mixing bowl. Stir water into meat mixture gradually, then add chopped cabbage and sesame oil.

Making the dumplings

Separate the wrappers and brush edges with water. Place about 1 tablespoon of filling in the center of each wrapper. Fold the wrapper in half to cover the filling and form a half moon shape. Pinch the edges together tightly to seal, starting from the center and moving to the sides. Repeat process until you have used up the filling. Refrigerate until ready to cook. The dumplings can be frozen on a tray, then transferred to a plastic bag or container. When you are ready to pan-fry the dumplings, there's no need to defrost them.

Cooking the dumplings

Heat a flat frying pan on medium-low heat until hot; add 2 tablespoons of oil and heat until hot. Add 20 to 25 dumplings to cover the bottom of the pan without overlapping. Fry dumplings until bottoms turn brown. Add ¼ cup of cold water, making sure to drench each dumpling. Turn to low heat, cover, and cook until water has evaporated (about 5 minutes). Uncover, turn heat slightly higher, add 1 tablespoon of oil, and let the dumplings fry 2 minutes longer. Serve with soy and vinegar sauce (see page 126), brown side up, allowing dumplings to remain stuck together in rows. (The frozen uncooked dumplings should be cooked 5 minutes longer after water is added.)

Makes about 100 small pot stickers or 70 large pot stickers.

POT STICKERS, VEGETARIAN
素鍋貼

Meat-filled pot stickers are popular in China as well as in the United States. I certainly don't want vegetarians to miss these delicious snacks, so I created this all-vegetable filling.

INGREDIENTS

½ pound firm tofu, minced
1 cup fresh mushrooms, minced
½ cup carrots, minced
½ cup bok choy, minced
¼ cup water chestnuts, minced
½ cup Chinese chives, minced
¼ cup Chinese parsley, minced
1 teaspoon ginger, minced
1 teaspoon garlic, minced

1 tablespoon soy sauce
½ teaspoon salt
¼ teaspoon white pepper
2 teaspoons sesame oil
2 packages round dumpling wrappers
   or 1 recipe Pot Sticker Wrappers
   (see page 140)
2 to 3 tablespoons oil

Making the filling

Drain and mince the tofu. Mince mushrooms, carrots, bok choy, water chestnuts, Chinese chives, Chinese parsley, ginger, and garlic. Combine tofu and vegetables in a medium-sized bowl. Add soy sauce, salt, white pepper, and sesame oil. Set aside.

Making the dumplings

Separate the wrappers and brush edges with water. Place about 1 tablespoon of filling in the center of each wrapper. Fold the wrapper in half to cover the filling and form a half moon shape. Pinch the edges together tightly to seal, starting from the center and moving to the sides. Repeat process until you have used up the filling. Refrigerate until ready to cook. The dumplings can be frozen on a tray, then transferred to a plastic bag or container. When you are ready to pan-fry the dumplings, there's no need to defrost them.

Cooking the dumplings

Heat a flat frying pan on medium-low heat until pan is hot. Add 2 tablespoons of oil. When oil is hot, add 20 to 25 dumplings to cover the bottom of the pan without overlapping. Fry dumplings until bottoms turn brown. Add ¼ cup of cold water, making sure to drench each dumpling. Turn to low heat, cover, and cook until water has evaporated (about 5 minutes). Uncover, turn heat slightly higher, add 1 tablespoon of oil, and let the dumplings fry 2 minutes longer. Serve with soy and vinegar sauce (see page 126), brown side up, allowing dumplings to remain stuck together in rows. (The frozen uncooked dumplings should be cooked 5 minutes longer after water is added.)

Makes about 80 small pot stickers or 40 large pot stickers.

POT STICKER WRAPPERS
鍋貼皮

The pot sticker dough can be made ahead of time and kept in a tightly covered container in the refrigerator for up to two days.

INGREDIENTS
4 cups all-purpose flour
½ teaspoon salt
1⅓ cups plus 1 to 2 tablespoons boiling water

Put the flour and salt into a large bowl and make a well in the center. Gradually add the boiling water, stirring with chopsticks to make a firm dough. Knead it until it feels smooth. Put the dough in the bowl and cover with a damp cloth. Let stand for 30 minutes.

Take a third of the dough and roll it into a long sausage shape, then cut into 1-inch pieces. Use your hand to flatten each round piece into a ¼-inch-thick piece. With a Chinese rolling pin, roll out each piece to form a circle about 3 inches in diameter.

Follow the same procedure with the rest of the dough.

Note: You can use a food processor to make this dough.

ROAST PORK STEAMED BUNS
叉燒飽

Everybody loves these buns. Even though this is a Cantonese snack, it's quite popular all over China. Nowadays when you go to a dim sum restaurant, these buns are one of the most popular items people will select. When I prepare this snack, I always make a large quantity. Once the buns have thoroughly cooled, freeze them for future use. To reheat, steam frozen buns for 10 minutes. You can also reheat frozen buns in the microwave. My good friend Ying Ling taught me how to wrap a wet paper towel around a bun and reheat it in the microwave to a desirable temperature.

INGREDIENTS
1 pound cooked Chinese roast pork (see page 28)
1 tablespoon garlic, minced
1 tablespoon oil
¼ cup toasted sesame seeds
1 recipe Basic Yeast Dough (page 124)

SEASONING SAUCE
3 tablespoons soy sauce
3 tablespoons oyster sauce
4 tablespoons sugar
1 tablespoon sesame oil
¼ teaspoon black pepper
2 tablespoons cornstarch
½ cup cold water

Cut the roast pork into very thin strips, then cut into ¼-inch pieces. Mince garlic. In a small bowl, combine seasoning sauce. Heat a wok or large skillet over medium-high heat until hot; add oil and heat until hot. Add garlic and stir briskly for 5 seconds. Add Chinese roast pork, stir-fry for 1 minute, then add seasoning sauce until the pork is coated evenly. Turn off the heat and sprinkle with toasted sesame seeds. Let the mixture cool. This is the filling.

Set up a steamer with two tiers. Divide the dough into 4 equal portions. Roll the dough into a sausage-shaped roll about 1½ inches in diameter. Slice roll into 1-inch pieces. With the palm of the hand, flatten each into a circle, then roll with a small rolling pin into a pancake 3½ to 4 inches in diameter. The center of each pancake should be thicker than the edge.

Put about 1 heaping tablespoon of filling in the center of each pancake. Pleat the edge around the filling, bringing the top folds together. Pinch and twirl them into a tiny knot. Repeat until all buns are made. Put each bun on a 2½-inch-square piece of waxed or parchment paper and set aside until the dough rises again (about 20 minutes). Bring the water in the steamer to a boil. Put the steamer tiers over the boiling water and steam the buns over high heat for 10 minutes. (Steam both tiers at one time.)

Makes about 40 to 45 small buns or 30 large buns.

SHAO MAI
燒賣

In Cantonese, shao mai means cook and sell. In the old days, these open-face dumplings traditionally were cooked and sold on the street; hence their name. They are delicious as appetizers or served for lunch with a salad or soup. Shao mai can be prepared ahead of time and kept frozen. Steam frozen uncooked shao mai for 15 minutes.

INGREDIENTS
1 pound ground pork
2 teaspoons ginger, minced
4 tablespoons green onion, minced
1 cup bamboo shoots or water chestnuts, chopped
1 tablespoon soy sauce
1 teaspoon salt
1 teaspoon sugar
1 tablespoon sesame oil
1 tablespoon rice wine
2 tablespoons cornstarch
2 tablespoons water
1 package round dumpling wrappers
    or 1 recipe Shao Mai Wrappers (see page 143)

Mince ginger and green onion. Chop bamboo shoots or water chestnuts. Combine the pork with ginger, soy sauce, salt, sugar, sesame oil, rice wine, cornstarch, and water. Stir the meat and seasoning in one direction until the mixture holds together. Add the green onion and bamboo shoots or water chestnuts, then mix. The filling is ready to be used.

While making the shao mai, cover the wrappers with a damp cloth to prevent them from drying. Place a wrapper in the palm of your hand and put 1 tablespoon of filling on the wrapper. Gather the sides of the wrapper around the filling, letting them pleat naturally. Squeeze the middle gently to make sure the wrapper fits firmly against the filling and to form a slight waist. Tap the dumpling lightly on the table to flatten the bottom and make it stand upright.

Arrange the shao mai in a ring in a steamer lined with a damp cloth. Steam for 10 minutes. Remove to a plate and serve. Serve with or without soy and vinegar sauce (see page 126).

Makes about 50 shao mai.

SHAO MAI WRAPPERS
燒賣皮

WONTON WRAPPERS
餛飩皮

These shao mai wrappers can also be used for homemade wonton wrappers when cut into squares. I must admit that I always prefer making homemade wrappers for pot stickers. Somehow they really taste extra good. But for making shao mai, I usually just buy ready-made wrappers. If you really want to give yourself a challenge, homemade wrappers definitely taste better. It is very helpful if you can use a food processor to knead the dough and a pasta machine to make the wrappers.

INGREDIENTS
3 cups all-purpose flour
½ teaspoon salt
3 eggs, well beaten
⅓ cup cold water (approximately)

Measure the flour and salt into a large bowl. Add beaten eggs and water to flour and salt. With chopsticks, mix the ingredients until they form a soft ball. Knead the dough in the bowl until it becomes smooth (about 4 minutes). Cover with a slightly damp cloth for at least 15 minutes.

Divide the dough in half. On a floured surface, roll the halves one at a time into a paper-thin sheet. To make shao mai wrappers, cut sheet into circles 3 to 4 inches in diameter. To make wonton wrappers, cut sheet into similar-sized squares. Sprinkle a little flour between the pieces and stack them. Cover with a slightly damp cloth. They are now ready to use.

Repeat this procedure with the other half of dough.

SHRIMP TOAST
蝦仁土司

Shrimp toast is quite popular on the Chinese dim sum menu. Most restaurants use the deep-frying method, but I have developed a simple way to make this appetizer by pan-frying. You can pan-fry the shrimp toast ahead of time, then keep it warm in the oven for 10 to 15 minutes. This finger food is ideal for cocktail parties.

INGREDIENTS

½ pound medium shrimp, chopped
1 large egg white
1 whole green onion, chopped
1 tablespoon fresh Chinese parsley,
   chopped
½ teaspoon salt
1 teaspoon cornstarch
2 teaspoons rice wine

½ teaspoon plus 2 tablespoons sesame oil
4 egg yolks
½ cup water
½ cup water chestnuts (about 8), chopped
8 slices dense white bread, crust removed
6 to 8 tablespoons oil
Chinese parsley, chopped (for garnish)

Wash shrimp if desired. Shell shrimp and remove the black vein. Dry with paper towels. Put the shrimp, egg white, green onion, Chinese parsley, salt, cornstarch, rice wine, and ½ teaspoon sesame oil in a food processor and pulse to finely chop. Process until just pureed. Transfer to a bowl. Add the water chestnuts to the shrimp mixture and mix until all the ingredients are combined. Put the egg yolks, the remaining 2 tablespoons sesame oil, and water in a shallow bowl and whisk to blend. Set aside.

Spread 2 tablespoons of the shrimp mixture onto each of 4 slices of bread. Top with the remaining 4 slices of bread. Press together gently but firmly. Heat oil in a large nonstick skillet over medium-high heat. Dip sandwiches in the egg mixture, coating them evenly on both sides. Fry until golden brown (about 4 minutes each side). Slice each sandwich into 2 triangles, place on a serving plate, and garnish with Chinese parsley.

Serves 5 to 6 people as an appetizer.

SPRING ROLLS
春卷

China is an agricultural country, where farmers make up the majority of the total population. Since spring is a busy farming season, when such important work as sowing and transplanting take place, the Chinese people attach great importance to the spring season. According to the Chinese lunar calendar, about a week after the Lunar New Year there is a period called Spring Begins. To the Chinese farming population, Spring Begins is even more important than the Lunar New Year. The spring roll is a special dish prepared by Chinese families during this period to worship their ancestors, entertain dinner guests, and celebrate the arrival of spring. Often spring rolls are given as presents on Spring Begins. The crisp bundles resemble gold bars and are offered in the hope that everyone will be prosperous and successful in the coming year. Spring rolls can be frozen after they have been fried slightly brown. Reheat in a preheated oven at 425 degrees for 20 to 25 minutes. Put spring rolls on a rack to reheat so they will be less greasy.

INGREDIENTS
1½ pounds boneless pork (preferably center cut boneless pork)
6 medium dried Chinese mushrooms, shredded
1 small green cabbage, shredded
1 medium carrot, shredded
1 cup bamboo shoots, shredded
1 cup celery, shredded
4 whole green onions, shredded
12 ounces fresh bean sprouts
6 tablespoons oil for stir-frying
1 teaspoon salt
½ teaspoon white pepper
Spring roll wrappers
½ cup cornstarch and ½ cup water to make a paste, or beaten egg with a little water
3 to 4 cups oil for deep-frying

MARINADE
3 tablespoons soy sauce
1 tablespoon cornstarch
1 tablespoon rice wine
⅛ teaspoon white pepper

In a bowl, mix marinade. Cut the pork with the grain into ⅛-inch-thick slices, then cut against the grain into 2-inch-long shreds and marinate for 20 to 30 minutes. Soak mushrooms in hot water for 20 minutes. Discard the water and squeeze the mushrooms dry. Cut off and discard mushroom stems, then cut each cap into ⅛-inch strips. Put all shredded vegetables in a large bowl with shredded mushrooms. Wash bean sprouts with cold water and drain well. Add to other vegetables and set aside.

Heat a wok or large skillet over high heat until hot; add 6 tablespoons of oil and heat until hot. Scatter in the pork and stir in fast motions to separate the shreds. Remove pork and drain. Bring a large pot of water to a boil and cook the vegetables for about 20 seconds. Drain well. Mix pork and vegetables in a large bowl, adding salt and white pepper.

Put 2 tablespoons of filling in a corner of a wrapper, 1 inch from the edge. With your hands, begin rolling into a cylinder about 4 inches long. Bring the two end flaps up over the top of the enclosed filling and press gently. Then continue to roll to the far point to form a neat roll. Moisten the far point with cornstarch paste, or beaten egg with a little water, to seal the roll. Place on plate with the sealed edge facing downward.

Heat a wok or large skillet over medium-high heat; add oil and heat to about 350 degrees. Deep-fry spring rolls until golden brown (about 4 to 5 minutes), turning them for even frying. Serve spring rolls with Chinese dipping sauces (see page 126).

Makes 50 extra large or 70 large spring rolls.

Helpful hints
Make 5 to 6 spring rolls and deep-fry them while you continue to make additional rolls. To avoid having the shredded meat sink to the bottom of the bowl, stir the filling occasionally to obtain an even meat and vegetable filling. When you have used about half the filling, drain off excess liquid; overly moist filling will soak the wrappers, causing them to break. Cool the deep-fried spring rolls completely before placing in a covered, airtight container to be frozen. Do not thaw the spring rolls before reheating.

Spring Rolls, Vegetarian
素春卷

I never met a vegetarian when I lived in Mainland China or Taiwan, although there are many of them, mostly Buddhist monks and nuns. I get many requests to teach private vegetarian cooking classes at students' homes. This is my own version of these meatless spring rolls. Spring rolls can be frozen after they have been fried slightly brown. Reheat in a preheated oven at 425 degrees for 20 to 25 minutes. Put spring rolls on a rack to reheat so they will be less greasy.

INGREDIENTS
1 cup portobello mushrooms, shredded
1 small green cabbage, shredded
1 cup Chinese chives, shredded
12 ounces fresh bean sprouts, shredded
1 medium carrot, shredded
1 cup bamboo shoots, shredded
1 cup celery, shredded
1½ teaspoons salt
½ teaspoon white pepper
Spring roll wrappers
½ cup cornstarch and ½ cup water to make
   a paste, or beaten egg with a little water
3 to 4 cups oil for deep-frying

SEASONING FOR MUSHROOMS
1 tablespoon soy sauce
1 tablespoon rice wine

Shred all vegetables, either by hand or using a food processor. Set aside.

Heat a wok or large skillet over high heat until hot; add 3 tablespoons of oil and heat until hot. Scatter in the mushrooms and stir in fast motions to separate the shreds. Cook until mushrooms are soft (about 4 to 5 minutes). Add the soy sauce and rice wine until well blended. Drain the mushrooms and set aside. Bring a large pot of water to a boil and cook all other vegetables for about 20 seconds. Drain well. Add salt, white pepper, and cooked mushrooms to the vegetable mixture and toss well.

Put 2 tablespoons of filling in a corner of a wrapper, 1 inch from the edge. With your hands, begin rolling into a cylinder about 4 inches long. Bring the two end flaps up over the top of the enclosed filling and press gently. Then continue to roll to the far point to form a neat roll. Moisten the far point with cornstarch paste, or beaten egg with a little water, to seal the roll. Place on plate with the sealed edge facing downward.

Heat a wok or large skillet over medium-high heat; add oil and heat to about 350 degrees. Deep-fry spring rolls until golden brown (about 4 to 5 minutes), turning them for even frying. Serve spring rolls with Chinese dipping sauces (see page 126).

Makes 50 extra large or 70 large spring rolls.

Helpful hints
Make 5 to 6 spring rolls and deep-fry them while you continue to make additional rolls. When you have used about half the filling, drain off excess liquid; overly moist filling will soak the wrappers, causing them to break. Cool the deep-fried spring rolls completely before placing in a covered, airtight container to be frozen. Do not thaw the spring rolls before reheating.

Sweet Snacks

ALMOND COOKIES
杏仁餅乾

My husband, friends, and students just love these simple and delicious cookies. I am very fond of making cookies in general, and I discovered that using an ice cream scoop to form the balls is a lot easier than rolling them by hand. It certainly speeds up the preparation time. These cookies are a great gift for your friends.

INGREDIENTS
2 cups all-purpose flour
1 teaspoon baking powder
½ teaspoon baking soda
1 cup shortening
⅔ cup brown sugar
½ cup sugar
1 egg
1 tablespoon almond extract
½ cup chopped almonds
¼ cup sesame seeds

Preheat oven to 375 degrees. Sift flour with baking powder and baking soda and set aside. In a large bowl, beat shortening with brown sugar and sugar until light and fluffy. Add egg and almond extract and beat until well blended. Add flour to creamed mixture and blend thoroughly to form soft dough. Add almonds and sesame seeds to dough until well blended.

Line 2 baking sheets with parchment paper or leave them ungreased. Measure out rounded teaspoonfuls of dough and roll them into balls with your hands. Place the balls about 1½ inches apart on the prepared baking sheet. Bake cookies until slightly brown (about 8 to 10 minutes). Immediately transfer to a rack to cool. When the cookies cool completely, store in an airtight container.

Makes about 40 cookies.

ALMOND FLOAT
杏仁豆腐

I was rather amused that my husband needed a sweet dessert after every meal when we were first married. In most Chinese families, fresh fruit is always served after a meal. As a matter of fact, when my family moved to Taiwan in 1949, we had all kinds of fruit trees growing in our backyard, such as guavas, dragon eyes, mangos, and papayas. When I came home from school, I usually picked the fruit from the trees. That was one of my fondest memories. In China, some families finish their meals with a sweet soup. A heavy dessert, such as Eight Precious Rice Pudding, is often served at festivals or banquets.

INGREDIENTS
2 packages unflavored gelatin
½ cup cold water
1⅓ cups sugar
1¼ cups boiling water
1½ cups table cream
1 tablespoon almond extract
1½ cups water

In a small bowl, sprinkle the gelatin over the cold water and let it set for 5 minutes. Add ⅓ cup sugar to 1¼ cups boiling water until it dissolves, then stir in softened gelatin. Add the cream and almond extract to the gelatin mixture. Pour the liquid into a shallow square or rectangular container and refrigerate until firm (about 4 hours). Combine remaining 1 cup sugar with 1½ cups water; cook over medium-high heat and stir to dissolve completely. Chill the sugar water in the refrigerator. Using a small knife, cut the almond float into square or diamond shapes. Lift them out with a spatula to a serving bowl. Pour the chilled sugar water over the individual pieces and serve cold.

Serves 5 to 6.

Note: Canned lychees, peeled fresh lychees, Mandarin orange sections, or other fresh fruit can be used as garnish.

CHINESE EGG TARTS
雞蛋撻

In my youth my snacks were mainly fresh fruits or sweet soups, such as green bean soup or red bean soup. I was formally introduced to egg tarts when I came to this country in 1964. Since Canton is close to the ocean and foreign influence is pervasive, the Cantonese created this egg custard-like dessert. It is tedious and time-consuming to make, but the result is really worthwhile. You can make the tarts ahead of time and store them in the freezer, then reheat them in a hot oven (400 degrees) for 5 to 8 minutes until warm. You'll need about 30 small tart pans for this recipe.

CRUST
2 cups all-purpose flour
3 tablespoons sugar
¼ teaspoon salt
2 sticks butter, sliced
¼ cup ice water or less

FILLING
1 cup sugar
1¼ cups milk
5 eggs, well beaten
1 teaspoon vanilla

Preheat oven to 375 degrees.

To prepare the crust: In a bowl of a food processor fitted with a steel blade, combine flour, sugar, and salt. Pulse a few times to mix. Add the butter and pulse and process until the mixture resembles coarse crumbs. Add the ice water all at once through the feed tube. Pulse until the mixture begins to form soft dough. Transfer to plastic wrap and chill for at least 1 hour.

Pull a small amount of dough (about 2 tablespoons) into a small tart pan. Using the thumb, gently press the pastry evenly into the pan, making sure to cover the bottom and side of the tart pan completely. Repeat for all tart pans.

In a small saucepan, add sugar and milk. Cook until the sugar dissolves. Set aside to cool. Beat eggs well, but not until frothy. Add beaten eggs to sugar and milk mixture. Add vanilla, stir, and pour through a fine strainer into tart pans. Put the tart pans on a large cookie sheet and bake for 30 minutes. Set them aside for 15 minutes, then invert the tarts. Serve warm, cold, or room temperature.

Makes about 30 small egg tarts.

CHINESE RICE PUDDING
八寶飯

Rice pudding is usually served at birthdays or wedding banquets in China. When I was growing up in China, rice pudding was one of my favorite treats. I usually tried not to stuff myself early with other gourmet food in order to save my appetite for this rich dessert. You can find red bean paste in any Chinese grocery store. This pudding can be prepared ahead of steaming time and kept refrigerated for two to three days. Alternatively, the pre-steamed pudding can be stored in the freezer and defrosted in the refrigerator or in the microwave before steaming.

INGREDIENTS
2 cups glutinous rice (sweet rice)
4 teaspoons sugar
4 teaspoons oil
¼ cup dried red dates
¼ cup sugared lotus seeds
¼ cup canned chestnuts, drained
¼ cup raisins
1 cup red bean paste

SAUCE
1 cup water
½ cup sugar
1 teaspoon vanilla
2 teaspoons cornstarch and 2 teaspoons
   water to make a paste

Wash rice well and soak in 2 cups of water for at least 2 hours. Drain well. Place rice in a steamer lined with a damp cloth and steam for 45 minutes. Turn off the heat and let rice stand for another 15 minutes. Mix cooked rice with sugar and oil in a bowl. Set aside.

In a small saucepan, soak the dried red dates in hot water for 10 minutes. Drain the water. Add ½ cup fresh water and cook the red dates over low heat for 20 minutes or in the microwave using medium-level power for 5 minutes. Use scissors to cut the dates in half and remove the seeds. Set aside.

Grease a 9-inch cake pan or a shallow bowl and line it with parchment paper. Grease the parchment paper. Arrange red dates, sugared lotus seeds, chestnuts, and raisins on the bottom of the pan or bowl. Add half the cooked rice on top of the dried fruit, pressing lightly to form a firm layer. Spread red bean paste over rice, then add a final layer of rice, using a greased spatula to pack down and smooth the layer.

Place the cake pan or bowl on the rack of a steamer and steam over medium-high heat for 1 hour. Near the end of the cooking time, bring water and sugar to a boil in a small saucepan, stirring until the sugar is dissolved. Add vanilla and cornstarch paste until the sauce is smooth. Keep warm.

Remove the pudding from the steamer with oven mitts and place a large plate over it. Invert onto plate. Peel off the parchment paper. Pour the sauce on top of the pudding.

Serves 6 to 8.

RED BEAN CAKE
紅豆糕

Chinese people have been eating red beans for many centuries. One of the reasons these beans are so popular is that they have a medicinal effect. That is why all herbal pharmacies in China sell red beans as one of their medications. When the climate is very humid, some people experience swollen, aching, or sore feet. According to a story told from generation to generation, if you eat two or three pieces of red bean cake every morning, all your health problems will be slowly cured. In the summer, I even freeze red bean cake and eat it like a popsicle treat.

INGREDIENTS
8 ounces dried red beans (adzuki beans)
1 to 2 cups sugar
2 packages unflavored gelatin
½ cup cold water

Wash and rinse the red beans well and drain. Soak the beans in cold water covering 1 inch above the beans for at least 3 hours or overnight. Drain again, add 4 cups of water, and bring to a boil, then simmer until the beans are well cooked (about 1 hour). There should be about 5 cups of beans and bean water left. Add sugar until it melts. In a small bowl, sprinkle the gelatin over ½ cup cold water and let it set for 5 minutes. Add the beans and bean water into the gelatin mixture and stir. Pour the bean mixture into a shallow square or rectangular container and refrigerate about 4 hours or until firm. Using a small knife, cut the bean cake into square or diamond shapes. You can serve the cake cold or at room temperature.

STEAMED SWEET RICE WITH COCONUT MILK
椰子糯米

My students really enjoy this light dessert. The best thing about this dish is that you can make it days or weeks ahead of time. During the Chinese New Year season, you can buy sweet lotus seeds (they are sold in a bag) and add them to the chestnuts and red dates. Before serving this dish, steam it for another 10 to 15 minutes, or for 30 minutes if frozen. Reheat individual pieces in the microwave for 15 to 20 seconds, or for 1 minute if frozen.

INGREDIENTS
2 cups glutinous rice (sweet rice)
1 cup dried red dates or raisins
½ cup brown sugar
½ cup water
1 can (13.5 ounces) coconut milk
1 bag (5.2 ounces) precooked chestnuts

TOPPING
1 cup unsweetened shredded coconut
½ cup confectioner's sugar

Wash rice well and soak in 2 cups of water for at least 2 hours. Drain well. Place the rice in a steamer lined with a damp cloth or parchment paper and steam for 45 minutes. Turn off the heat and let rice stand for another 15 minutes.

In a small saucepan, soak the dried red dates in boiling water for 15 minutes. Drain the water, then use scissors to cut the dates in half and remove the seeds. Set aside. If you use raisins, soak in hot water for 10 minutes and drain. Combine brown sugar and water; cook over medium-high heat and stir to dissolve completely.

Place steamed rice into a medium saucepan. Add coconut milk, chestnuts, red dates or raisins, and sugar water. Stir over low heat until the coconut milk has been completely absorbed (about 6 minutes). Line an 8-inch x 8-inch baking pan with parchment paper. Spread the rice on top evenly. Set in the refrigerator until firm (about 2 hours). Remove from the refrigerator, place baking pan and rice in the steamer, and steam for another 30 minutes.

While the coconut rice is being steamed, prepare the topping. Scatter shredded coconut on a large cookie sheet and bake in a 300-degree oven until brown (about 5 to 8 minutes). When the toasted coconut has cooled off, add confectioner's sugar.

Remove the coconut rice from the steamer. When cool, cut into small squares with a buttered knife. Just before serving, steam for another 10 to 15 minutes. Sprinkle with toasted shredded coconut topping.

Makes 16 pieces.

SWEET NEW YEAR CAKE
甜年糕

In China, the biggest holiday is Lunar New Year. When I was a child we could not buy ready-made glutinous rice powder, so my mother had to soak the glutinous rice overnight. The next day she would use a stone grinder to manually grind the rice into a very fine mixture with water. I am still very fond of this cake, especially when slices are fried in oil and sprinkled with powered sugar. Glutinous rice powder and bamboo leaves can be bought in Asian supermarkets.

INGREDIENTS
3 cups glutinous rice powder
3 to 4 bamboo leaves or parchment paper
1 cup brown sugar
1 cup water
Oil for brushing

Soak the bamboo leaves for several hours and keep soaking until ready to use. Bring sugar and water to a boil. When the sugar is dissolved and the liquid cools off, add glutinous rice powder to the mixture. Stir well with chopsticks or electric mixer until smooth.

Wipe the bamboo leaves dry with paper towels and brush them with oil. Line a springform pan with the bamboo leaves, making sure that the leaves cover the inside of the pan, or line with parchment paper. Pour the rice batter into the pan. Fill a large steamer pot with 2 gallons of water and bring the water to a boil. Place the pan on the rack of a steamer and steam for 2 hours. Let the rice cake cool for 30 minutes. Peel off the bamboo leaves. The cake is ready to eat.

Variation
Alternatively, you can let the cake cool completely, then slice it, beat 2 eggs, dip the slices in the beaten eggs, pan-fry them in oil, and serve. You can add cooked red beans, cooked lotus seeds, Chinese dates, and broken walnut pieces to the rice batter before steaming.

Makes one rice cake.

SWEET RICE CAKE WITH LOTUS SEEDS
蓮子糯米糕

Asian people just love to eat sweet rice, although this glutinous rice is not sweet at all when you purchase it in the market. So many sweet, heavy snacks are made from glutinous rice that most companies decided to translate the name to sweet rice. In China we don't usually serve dessert after a meal, only fresh fruit. But we do eat lots of sweet rice snacks between meals. I make this snack quite often and freeze the cakes individually. When I have the urge, I put a piece in the microwave for 1 minute. Yummy!

INGREDIENTS
2 cups glutinous rice (sweet rice)
½ cup dried red dates or raisins
1 cup sugar
6 ounces sweet lotus seeds

Wash rice well and soak in 2 cups of water for at least 2 hours. Drain well. Place the rice in a steamer lined with a damp cloth or parchment paper and steam for 45 minutes. Turn off the heat and let rice stand for another 15 minutes.

In a small saucepan, soak the dried red dates in boiling water for 15 minutes. Drain the water, then use scissors to cut the dates in half and remove the seeds. Set aside. If you use raisins, soak in hot water for 10 minutes and drain.

In a medium-sized heatproof bowl, add sugar into hot rice and mix well. Add lotus seeds and red dates and stir until they are evenly distributed. Steam for another 30 minutes.

Remove the hot rice mixture. Line a 9-inch x 9-inch baking pan with parchment paper. Spread the rice mixture on top evenly. When the rice cake has cooled, cut into small squares or diamond shapes to serve. Just before serving, steam for another 5 minutes.

Makes 16 pieces.

SWEET RICE CAKE WITH SHREDDED COCONUT
椰絲糯米糕

Most Chinese people just never seem to get enough snacks made from glutinous rice and glutinous rice powder. Coconut rice cake is quite popular among the Chinese. When you store it in the refrigerator, the cake will get hard and stiff. You can steam it again for a few minutes, or put it in the microwave for a few seconds until it softens. If you don't like coconut, simply omit it and the rice cake still tastes great. You can find red bean paste in any Chinese grocery store.

INGREDIENTS
2½ cups glutinous rice powder
3 tablespoons wheat starch
1 tablespoon butter
½ cup boiling water
1 cup cold water
1½ cups red bean paste
10 whole maraschino cherries, cut in half

TOPPING
1 cup unsweetened shredded coconut
½ cup confectioner's sugar

Put the wheat starch and butter in a medium-sized bowl and stir in the boiling water with a wooden spoon or chopsticks until smooth. Add the glutinous rice powder to the wheat starch mixture, then slowly add the cold water until the dough is well blended. Knead the dough for another 2 minutes. Take half of the dough and roll it into a long sausage shape, then cut it into 1-inch pieces. Shape each piece into a ball, then use your thumb to make a deep cup. Fill the cup with 1½ teaspoons of red bean paste and close the cup by pressing the edge to seal. Lightly press down each piece with the palm of your hand to form a 2-inch circle. Follow the same procedure with the rest of the dough.

Put all the uncooked rice cakes in a greased metal steamer and steam for 10 minutes. While the rice cakes are being steamed, prepare the topping. Scatter shredded coconut on a large cookie sheet and bake in a 300-degree oven until brown (about 5 to 8 minutes). When the toasted coconut has cooled, add confectioner's sugar.

Remove the rice cakes immediately from steamer and coat them with topping. Garnish each cake with a piece of cherry. Serve hot, warm, or at room temperature.

Makes 20 cakes.

SWEET WALNUTS OR PECANS
甜核桃

Nuts are not cheap in China. They are often served at banquets as a first course with cold meat or with seafood. When I was growing up in Taiwan, I don't recall that my mother ever prepared this dish for us. Since baking in the oven is uncommon in China, this dish is typically deep-fried. I have been experimenting for some time to come up with a baking method, and I am quite pleased with the result. One benefit of baking as opposed to deep-frying is that the number of calories is greatly reduced. Sweet walnuts, pecans, and almonds are great for snacks and for adding to your stir-fried dishes. The most wonderful way to serve these nuts is as toppings for ice cream. The nuts make nice gifts during the holiday season.

INGREDIENTS
1 pound shelled walnut halves or pecan halves (about 4 cups)
1½ cups sugar
1½ cups water
2 tablespoons oil

In a large pot, bring 4 cups of water to a boil. Add the nuts and cook on medium-high heat for 5 minutes, stirring every 2 to 3 minutes. Drain and rinse with cold water; drain again. (The dark skin of the walnuts is a little bitter; you can peel them with tweezers, if you wish. I find this too tedious.)

Mix sugar and water in a medium-sized pot over medium-high heat, stirring to dissolve the sugar. Add walnuts or pecans, reduce the heat to low, and simmer for 10 minutes, stirring every 2 to 3 minutes. Remove the pot and let the nuts cool in the syrup for another 10 minutes.

Preheat oven to 300 degrees. Drain the nuts and transfer them to a large bowl. Add the oil and mix them well. Grease a large baking pan and spread the nuts evenly on it. Bake for 18 to 20 minutes.

Variation
You can substitute whole almonds for walnuts or pecans. Boil the almonds in water for 2 minutes, then drain and rinse with cold water. Peel the skin off the almonds with your fingers. Follow the same method above to sweeten the almonds.

SWEET WONTONS
甜餛飩

Everyone knows about wonton soup and fried wontons, but most people have seldom heard of sweet wontons. Since an oven did not exist in the Chinese kitchen when I was a youngster, many sweet snacks were made by deep-frying. Ready-made wonton wrappers are easily found in Asian supermarkets. These sweet wontons are simple to make and are a great gift for all occasions.

INGREDIENTS
1 pound square wonton wrappers
3 cups oil for deep-frying
4 tablespoons confectioner's sugar

FILLING
½ pound pitted dates
½ cup chopped nuts (any kind)
1 tablespoon grated fresh lemon zest or
  orange zest
¼ cup toasted sesame seeds, black or white
2 tablespoons lemon juice or orange juice

Chop dates with a cleaver or food processor. Chop nuts with a cleaver. Grate the lemon with a zester. Heat a frying pan on medium-low heat until hot. Stir-fry sesame seeds without oil until lightly brown. In a small bowl, combine dates, nuts, lemon zest or orange zest, sesame seeds, and lemon juice or orange juice until they are nicely mixed.

Place about 1 teaspoon of filling on one corner of wrapper, then roll toward the opposite corner, squeezing the filling into a cylinder shape. Keep rolling until about ½ inch from the opposite corner. Moisten corner with water and seal. Then hold the wonton in both hands and twist ends in opposite directions.

Heat a wok or large skillet over medium-high heat; add 3 cups oil. Deep-fry the sweet wontons at 375 degrees until golden brown and crispy. Scoop out wontons with a large skimmer and place on paper towels. Just before serving, sprinkle wontons with confectioner's sugar. Serve hot or at room temperature.

Makes about 45 to 50 sweet wontons.

WALNUT COOKIES
核桃餅乾

My mother never made cookies for us when we were growing up in Taiwan. There was simply no oven in the kitchen. Nowadays toaster ovens and microwave ovens are quite popular in China, but regular ovens are still quite rare in most households, so cookies and pastries are usually purchased at the bakery. If you don't like to bake, you can find ready-made cookies in Chinese grocery stores and bakeries.

INGREDIENTS
1¾ cups all-purpose flour
1 teaspoon baking powder
½ teaspoon baking soda
1 cup shortening
⅔ cup brown sugar
½ cup sugar
1 egg
1 teaspoon vanilla
¼ cup finely chopped walnuts
Toasted sesame seeds
About 40 walnut halves

Sift flour with baking powder and baking soda and set aside. In a large bowl, beat shortening with brown sugar and sugar until fluffy. Add egg and vanilla and beat until well blended. Add flour mixture to creamed mixture and blend thoroughly to form soft dough. Add chopped walnuts and mix well. Divide the dough into several sausage rolls about 1½ inches in diameter. Chill the dough for 2 to 3 hours.

Preheat oven to 350 degrees. With a sharp knife, cut the chilled dough crosswise into ½-inch slices. Roll in sesame seeds to coat evenly. Put slices on an ungreased baking sheet, side by side and 1 inch apart. Press a piece of walnut in the center of each disk. Bake cookies until slightly brown (about 8 to 10 minutes). Immediately transfer to a rack to cool. When the cookies cool completely, store in an airtight container.

Makes about 40 cookies.

CHINESE INGREDIENTS

Baby corn 小粟米
This tiny vegetable is also called young corn. Baby corn is used mostly in stir-fried foods, or as a garnish. The whole corn is edible. Once the can is opened, the baby corn should be stored in fresh water in a covered container and refrigerated. If the water is changed every other day, the corn will last ten days to two weeks.

Bamboo shoots 竹筍
There are three kinds of bamboo shoots: winter bamboo shoots, spring bamboo shoots, and summer bamboo shoots. It is difficult to find fresh ones in Asian supermarkets in the United States. There are plenty of canned bamboo shoots, which come pre-sliced, shredded, or whole. Once the can is opened, the bamboo shoots should be stored in fresh water in a covered container and refrigerated. If the water is changed every other day, the shoots will last ten days to two weeks.

Bean curd (tofu) 豆腐
A protein-rich food coagulated from an extract of soybeans, bean curd is used in various cooked foods and salads. It is called tofu by the Japanese and doufu by the Chinese. You can buy fresh bean curd in Asian supermarkets, but you must keep it in water and change the water every other day. There are three kinds of bean curds: silken, regular, and firm. Silken bean curd is usually used in salad dressings and desserts. Regular and firm bean curds are used in stir-fried dishes and soup. Nowadays you can buy bean curd in tubs and cartons; it is pasteurized and has an expiration date. Unused bean curd should be stored in fresh water in a covered container and refrigerated. If the water is changed every other day, the bean curd will last for up to a week.

Bean curd, pressed (pressed tofu) 豆腐乾
When water is pressed out of firm bean curd, it is called pressed bean curd. There are two kinds of pressed bean curd: plain 白豆腐乾 and seasoned 五香. The latter is cooked in soy sauce and star anise to give it a brown color. Check the package for the expiration date.

Bean curd, pressed and shredded (pressed and shredded tofu) 乾豆腐絲
This is pressed bean curd (either plain or seasoned) that has been shredded. It is sold in plastic bags. Check the package for the expiration date.

Bean curd, pressed and smoked (pressed and smoked tofu) 燻豆腐乾
This is pressed bean curd (either plain or seasoned) that has been smoked. It is sold in plastic bags. Check the package for the expiration date.

Bean curd puffs (fried tofu) 油豆腐
Hard bean curds, cut into 1½-inch cubes and deep-fried in oil until golden brown on the outside, are called bean curd puffs (fried tofu). Packaged in plastic bags and sold by weight or sold as loose puffs in large tubs in some Asian supermarkets, they are used in making stews or stuffed with meat or seafood. They will keep in the refrigerator for a week.

Bean curd sheet (tofu sheet) 豆腐衣
This is the same as tofu skin (next entry), except that the skin is much thinner. It comes in a 26-inch round shape and can be bought in the frozen department of Chinese grocery stores.

Bean curd skin (tofu skin) 百頁

When soybean milk is cooked and heated, a film forms on top of the liquid, just like when you boil milk or cream. Bean curd sheets are made from this film. You can buy fresh ones in the refrigerated section of Asian supermarkets. Check the package for the expiration date.

Bean paste, sweet and red 紅豆沙

This sweet, red bean paste is made from mashed red beans and sugar. It can be homemade or ready-made. The latter is sold in cans. Once the can is opened, transfer the paste to a tightly sealed container and keep in the refrigerator for up to weeks, or in the freezer indefinitely. It is used for sweet snacks such as Chinese Rice Pudding.

Bean sauce, hot 辣豆瓣醬

This is a very important ingredient for Sichuan cooking. Many companies make this product. I choose the one made in Sichuan Province. Transferred from the can to a tightly sealed container, it keeps indefinitely in the refrigerator.

Bean sprouts 豆芽

Grown from mung beans, you can buy them in Asian supermarkets as well as American supermarkets in the United States. If you change the water every other day, the bean sprouts will keep for one week in the refrigerator.

Black beans, fermented 豆豉

Small, soft, salty, and fermented, black beans have a very pungent smell and are used for cooking bland food, such as bean curd dishes and steamed dishes. They can be bought in small plastic bags, in jars, or in cans. They can be stored in a tightly sealed container in the refrigerator for a very long period of time.

Cabbages: green cabbage 包心菜, napa cabbage 天津大白菜, bok-choy 白菜

Everyone is familiar with green cabbage. Napa cabbage, also called celery cabbage, originally came from Northern China. It can be used in stir-frying or making soup. Since the stalks are a little tougher, cook them first until they are almost translucent, then add the leaves. Bok-choy, which means Chinese cabbage in Cantonese, is a loose-leafed cabbage with thick white stalks and dark green leaves. It is good for cooking and stewing but cannot be eaten raw. Refrigerate all types for up to a week.

Cassia blossoms, preserved 桂花醬

The cassia blossom is a tiny, yellow, four-petaled flower with a pleasant fragrance. The blossoms are collected and preserved in sugar and salt. They are sold in small bottles and used for flavoring sweet dishes. After the bottle has been opened, the blossoms will keep in the refrigerator for up to a year.

Cellophane noodles 粉絲

Also known as bean thread noodles and transparent vermicelli, cellophane noodles are made from ground mung beans. The noodles are sold in dried bundles weighing a few ounces to a pound and stored in plastic packages. You must soak the noodles in hot water to soften before adding to the dish. Use a pair of scissors to cut them into shorter lengths after soaking, since the noodles are very long. Keep the packages in a cool, dry place. Cellophane noodles will keep for a long time.

Chestnuts 栗子

Fresh, dried, canned, and ready-to-eat chestnuts are available in Asian supermarkets, but the fresh and ready-to-eat ones can be purchased only during the holiday season. Cut a crisscross in the flat side of fresh chestnuts, then immerse completely in water and boil for 10 minutes. Peel them right away. Dried chestnuts must be soaked in boiling water for at least one hour before they can be used for cooking.

Chili oil 辣椒油

Chili oil is a must for preparing Sichuan dishes. People who love a fiery taste in their food may wish to add it to salads, soups, stir-fried dishes, and dim sum dipping sauces by mixing chili oil with soy sauce. Chili oil can be purchased in all Asian supermarkets. To make homemade chili oil, heat 1 cup of oil in a small saucepan until hot, add ¼ cup of crushed red pepper flakes, and stir for 20 seconds. Turn off the heat; let the oil steep for several hours until cool. Use a coffee filter to strain the oil and keep it in a small bottle with a tight cap. Store the chili oil in the refrigerator for up to several months.

Chili paste or sauce 辣椒醬

Chili paste or sauce is popular among the Chinese, Vietnamese, and Thai people. The degree of fieriness depends on the makers. This sauce is made with crushed fresh chili peppers and salt. Additional ingredients such as vinegar, ginger, garlic, soy sauce, toasted Sichuan peppercorn powder, soybeans, and sesame oil can be mixed in with the sauce. Once a can of chili paste or sauce has been opened, the paste or sauce can be transferred to an airtight container and kept in the refrigerator indefinitely.

Chinese broccoli 芥蘭

Chinese broccoli is completely different from American broccoli. The former has a thin, long stem with green leaves and tiny flowers. It tastes a little bitter, so sugar is often added to neutralize the flavor. Fresh broccoli will keep in the refrigerator for up to a week.

Chinese chives 韭菜

There are three kinds of Chinese chives in Asian supermarkets: green chives, yellow chives, and flowering chives. They all need to be cut into 1½-inch lengths before use in stir-frying. Minced green chives are often used in making dim sum fillings. Refrigerate fresh chives for up to a week.

Chinese ham 火腿

Chinese ham is as famous as Virginia Smithfield ham. Both have almost the same taste, texture, and color. Since the ham has an excellent flavor, it is used both as a garnish and as a main course. It will keep for several weeks in the refrigerator if tightly wrapped in foil or plastic.

Chinese jujubes (red dates) 紅棗

Jujubes come from the northern part of China. They are green when fresh, reddish brown when dried. Only the dried ones can be found in the United States. You must soak them in hot water to soften the texture. Store in a tightly sealed container in the refrigerator or freezer. Many Chinese people believe that eating jujubes treats anxiety, insomnia, and dizziness.

Chinese New Year candies 新年糖果

Sweetened lotus roots, sweetened carrot slices, sweetened winter melon slices, and sweetened lotus seeds are all popular candies served during the Chinese New Year. Whether you live in the United States or in China, this is a tradition among all the Chinese.

Chinese noodles 麵

Chinese noodles can be fresh or dried, with egg or without. In China, northerners consume more noodles than rice, since wheat is grown more abundantly in the north than is rice. The best noodles are fresh egg noodles, which can be bought in all Asian supermarkets. Store fresh noodles in the refrigerator for up to a week, or freeze them for up to several months. Dried egg noodles stored in a tightly sealed container in a cool, dry place will keep for months.

Chinese parsley (fresh coriander or cilantro) 芫茜

This aromatic and distinctive herb with flat leaves has a stronger flavor than Italian parsley. Chinese parsley is used mainly for garnish. To store, place parsley upright in a glass of water with the roots attached and cover loosely with a plastic bag. It will stay fresh in the refrigerator for up to ten days.

Chinese sausages 臘腸

Once made only from pork and pork fat, nowadays the majority of Chinese sausages are made from chicken, duck, and beef. Chinese sausages must be either steamed or boiled before being eaten. The sausages are available in vacuum-sealed packages. Store in the refrigerator for up to a month or in the freezer for several months.

Coconut milk 椰奶

Making coconut milk from a fresh coconut is a big challenge and time consuming. Coconut milk is sold in Asian and Latin American stores. Chinese people use coconut milk mainly for making desserts, such as coconut sweet rice. Refrigerate coconut milk for up to a few days or freeze for future use.

Curry powder 咖喱粉

Curry powder is a mixture of turmeric, cumin, red pepper, cinnamon, ginger, garlic, coriander, fenugreek, cardamom, fennel, star anise, clove, allspice, and nutmeg. Buying ready-made curry powder is easier than mixing your own. Prepared curry powders are available in cans, jars, and bottles of various sizes. Store curry powder in a cool, dry place, and it will keep for months.

Five-spice powder 五香粉

This is a very strong spice made from five different powders: ground anise, cinnamon, cloves, fennel, and ginger. Nowadays, five-spice powder may include a few more ingredients: licorice, toasted Sichuan peppercorn powder, and dried tangerine peel. Different brands have different combinations of spices and may vary in aroma and taste. Sprinkle five-spice powder over poultry or pork to make the meat more flavorful. The powder is sold ready-mixed in small plastic packages or in a small jar. It will keep for a year at room temperature in a tightly sealed container.

Ginger 薑

You can find this knobby brown root in all supermarkets. Choose a root that is smooth and firm. When a recipe calls for a slice of ginger, it means a piece of ginger about 1 inch in diameter and $1/8$ inch thick. Remove the skin with a peeler, or better yet with a spoon. Slice, shred, or mince ginger, and use it to enhance meat, poultry, seafood, and vegetables dishes. It is not necessary to peel ginger if it is used only for flavoring. To make ginger juice, mince the ginger finely, wrap in a strong paper towel, and squeeze out the juice. Two tablespoons of minced ginger produce one teaspoon of ginger juice. Ginger that has been peeled and minced should be stored in a tightly sealed container and will keep in the refrigerator for one week to ten days. Unpeeled ginger stored in a tightly sealed container or plastic bag will keep in the refrigerator for weeks.

Hair seaweed 髮菜

Hair seaweed is almost black and looks like hair. In the Mandarin dialect, the Chinese word for hair seaweed sounds like "making a fortune" 發財, so the Chinese love to serve this dish for good luck. Even though hair seaweed has little flavor, it gives a unique presentation to certain dishes. It must be soaked first.

Hoisin sauce 海鮮醬

This sweet, chocolate-like sauce is made from soybeans, sugar, water, vinegar, garlic, and flour. It is used at the table or in cooking. Hoisin sauce often accompanies Mandarin pancakes served with Moo

Shi Pork and Peking Duck. It's also used for making Chinese roast pork. Hoisin sauce is available in cans and bottles. After opening the container, the sauce should be kept in the refrigerator with a tight cover. It will keep for up to a year.

Hot mustard 芥末

Hot mustard is served as a condiment for deep-fried appetizers such as spring rolls and fried wontons in all Chinese restaurants and at home. Chinese hot mustard made from English mustard powder diluted with water has the most satisfying taste. Measure an equal amount of powder and water and keep stirring until it becomes a smooth paste. A variety of prepared mustards are available in bottles and jars. Tightly covered, the loose powder and prepared mustard will keep in the refrigerator for months.

Kohlrabi 球莖甘藍

Also called turnip-steamed cabbage. In appearance, however, kohlrabi is quite distinct from cabbage. It has a rounded stem, somewhat similar to the turnip. After removing the skin from kohlrabi with a peeler, it is crisp and chewy and great for stir-frying and making salads. Store kohlrabi in a tightly sealed container or plastic bag and refrigerate. It will keep for weeks.

Lotus leaves, dried 乾荷葉

Lotus leaves are not for eating in China but instead are used exclusively for wrapping food such as rice, fish, meat, and poultry before steaming. The lotus leaves emit a distinctive flavor to the food being steamed. They are sold in plastic packages and measure almost 2 feet in diameter. Dried lotus leaves must be softened by soaking them in hot water for at least 30 minutes. Dried lotus leaves can be kept for months in a cool, dry place. Unused, already softened leftover lotus leaves can be stored in the freezer for future use.

Lotus seeds 蓮子

Lotus seeds are available in dried form, ready-to-eat, and in cans. Generally, dried lotus seeds need to be soaked or boiled until they are soft. They are used mainly in sweet soups and desserts. Once a can is opened, the seeds should be transferred to another container, soaked in water, and kept in the refrigerator. They will last for a week if you change the water every other day.

Lychees 荔枝

Lychees are a popular Chinese fruit that can be bought dried, fresh, or in cans. Dried lychees are available in plastic bags and are usually eaten as a snack – just as Americans eat raisins, dates, and prunes – or are added to sweet desserts. Remove the brittle shell, eat the dehydrated pulp inside, and discard the large pit. Fresh lychees are small and round with a rough shell, white pulp inside, and a large pit. Fresh lychees are naturally sweet and available in the United States in the summer in some Asian supermarkets. Canned lychees are sweet and packed in syrup, without shells or pits. Chilled lychees are served with cold almond float or other fruit salads. After opening the can, store the lychees in their own syrup in a tightly sealed container and keep in the refrigerator for up to several days.

Mung bean sheets 粉皮

Round mung bean sheets are the same as cellophane noodles. Both are made from ground mung beans with water. Both noodles and sheets become translucent after soaking in boiling water. Soak cellophane noodles for 10 minutes and mung bean sheets for 30 minutes. Mung bean sheets are sold in stacks packed in plastic bags. Store them in a tightly sealed container or plastic bag and keep in a cool, dry place for as long as a year. Discard them when they begin to smell rancid.

Mushrooms, dried Chinese 冬菇

Chinese mushrooms range from the size of a quarter to 3 inches in diameter. They have a rich, meat flavor and a wide flat cap, and they add color to many dishes. Dried mushrooms must be soaked in hot water at least 20 minutes to bring them back to their original shape. Drain, squeeze out the water, and cut off the stems. The water used in soaking can be saved for adding to soups or sauces. The mushrooms are sold in Asian supermarkets by weight or already packaged. Store in a cool, dry place for months or in the freezer indefinitely.

Mushrooms, straw 草菇

Straw mushrooms are different in texture and flavor from other mushrooms. They are sold in cans and have a meaty taste. Unused straw mushrooms should be stored in water in a tightly sealed container and refrigerated. They will keep for a week if you change the water every other day.

Mushrooms, wood ears 木耳

Wood ears, tree ears, cloud ears, and black fungus are all mushrooms with different names. Choose wood ears that are small and thin rather than large and thick. Soak wood ears in hot water for 30 minutes to soften before use. Wood ears used in most Chinese dishes are cut into thin strips. In recent years, dried shredded wood ears have become available in plastic packages in most Asian supermarkets, so they require no shredding. Wood ears stored in a tightly sealed container or plastic bag in a cool, dry place will keep for months.

Oil 油

The only oil we used for stir-frying in China when I was young was lard. Oil for use in Chinese cooking should be odorless, tasteless, and clear. Since butter will burn and smoke in high temperatures and olive oil is too strong for Chinese cooking, I recommend any of the following vegetable oils: peanut oil, corn oil, soybean oil, or canola oil.

Orange peels, dried 陳皮

Both dried orange peels and dried tangerine peels are used for soups and sauces in Chinese cooking. Sun-dried orange peels are sold in plastic packages. Before using, soak the peels in warm water until softened. Once opened, dried peels should be stored in the same plastic package in a cool, dry place. They will keep for months.

Oyster-flavored sauce 蠔油

This thick, brown, chocolate-like sauce is made from oyster extracts, sugar, seasoning, and cornstarch. Vegetarian oyster-flavored sauce, also called vegetarian mushroom flavored sauce, is now available in Asian supermarkets. It is made from mushroom extracts, sugar, soy sauce, and cornstarch. It is especially good in stir-fried beef and chicken dishes. Some people use it as a dipping sauce. Oyster-flavored sauce is very salty; once opened, it will keep for a long time in the refrigerator.

Red beans (adzuki beans) 紅豆

We Chinese love beans and especially sweet red bean paste made from red beans. Red beans are used to make many sweet, heavy snacks, such as red bean cake and sweet rice cake with shredded coconut. They are also used to make one of my favorite snacks, sweet red bean soup. Red beans are sold by weight in plastic bags and can be purchased at all Asian supermarkets.

Rice, crispy 鍋巴

When you boil rice too long in the pot, a thin, hard crust will form at the bottom of the pot. This hard crust can be air-dried and deep-fried to make homemade crispy rice. Nowadays, you can buy ready-made crispy rice. If it is already deep-fried, simply reheat it in a 425-degree oven for 10 minutes before adding to your favorite soup. Crispy rice is packaged in plastic bags containing 15 to 20 pieces each. Be careful: sometimes the rice isn't pre-deep-fried, so you have to deep-fry it yourself. Any leftover crispy rice is best stored in the freezer, where it will keep for many months.

Rice flour 粘米粉
Rice flour is made from ground long-grain rice and is used in making some dim sum dishes. It is sold in one-pound bags. Store in a tightly sealed container in a cool, dry place.

Rice flour, glutinous 糯米粉
Glutinous rice flour is made from ground glutinous rice. It is the main ingredient for making Chinese New Year cake and some dim sum dishes. Glutinous rice flour is sold in one-pound bags. Store in a tightly sealed container in a cool, dry place.

Rice, glutinous (sweet rice) 糯米
This round, short-grain rice is essential for making savory stuffing, pearl balls, rice pudding, sweet coconut rice, etc. You must wash the rice thoroughly and soak in water for at least 2 hours. When glutinous rice is cooked, it becomes soft, sticky, and translucent. It is sold by weight in bags. Store the rice in a tightly sealed container in a cool, dry place.

Rice, long-grain 粘米
Rice is one of the most basic foods in China. Long-grain rice is less starchy after being cooked and is ideal for making fried rice. Store rice in a tightly sealed container in a cool, dry place. Cooked rice can be stored in the refrigerator for several days, or in the freezer for months. Check the package to see if the rice should be washed.

Rice, medium-grain 中米
Medium-grain rice is shorter than long-grain rice. It is very popular in eastern and southern China. It's a little sticky, which is why the Japanese use it to make sushi. Store as you would store long-grain rice (see above). Check the package to see if the rice should be washed.

Rice noodles, dried 米粉
Rice noodles, also called rice sticks, are made from long-grain rice flour. There are many types of rice noodles with different widths and lengths. These noodles do not need to be parboiled, only soaked in warm water to soften. Rice noodles can be stir-fried, deep-fried, or used directly in soups. They come in one-pound packages, rolled in tight wads. Store rice noodles in a tightly sealed container in a cool, dry place. They will keep for months.

Rice noodles, fresh 河粉
Fresh rice noodles are made from long-grain flour. They are soft and milky white noodles which you can buy in folded sheets or in wide or narrow strips. They are coated with a thin layer of oil to prevent them from sticking together. You can find them in the refrigerated section of Asian supermarkets. It is ideal to cook fresh rice noodles the same day you buy them. Fresh rice noodles can be kept in the refrigerator for a few days, but they will become stiff. Rinse them in boiling water before cooking, and they will become soft again.

Rice vinegar 米醋
Rice vinegar is milder and less pungent than American white vinegar. Since I learned Chinese cooking in Japan, I have been using Japanese rice vinegar for a long time. I use the type of rice vinegar with no sodium and no sugar.

Rice wine 米酒

The most famous rice wine for Chinese cooking is from Shaoxing 紹興, a city in eastern China, so Shaoxing rice wine (also spelled Shao Hsing or Shaohsing) is my choice. When rice wine is not available, substitute pale-dry sherry. Store rice wine in a cool, dry place, and it will keep for months.

Rock sugar 冰糖

Rock sugar is crystallized sugar which is used in braised meat dishes and in making sauces. It brings a slightly sweet flavor and a glossy appearance to dishes. Prepare rock sugar for measuring by putting it in a strong plastic bag and crushing it with a mallet into small pieces. Rock sugar is sold in plastic packages. Store in a tightly sealed container in a cool, dry place, and it will keep for months.

Sesame oil 蔴油

Sesame oil is made from toasted sesame seeds and is quite different from the kind you see in Middle Eastern stores, which is made from raw sesame seeds. Sesame oil has a strong, nutlike flavor and therefore is not suitable for use as cooking oil. Generally, it is used for flavoring sauces, salads, and soups. A few drops of sesame oil also enhance the taste and aroma of hot dishes. Stored in a cool, dry place, sesame oil will keep for months.

Sesame seed paste 芝蔴醬

Sesame seed paste is made from toasted white sesame seeds. It usually comes in a jar combined with oil. The paste tends to settle at the bottom of the jar, so you have to stir it really well with a pair of chopsticks or a spoon until it becomes smooth. It is used primarily to make dressings for cold dishes. It is a common ingredient in Northern and Sichuan cooking. Middle Eastern tahini, made from untoasted white sesame seeds, can be substituted, but I prefer using creamy peanut butter mixed with sesame oil. An opened jar of sesame paste will keep in the refrigerator for several months.

Sesame seeds 芝蔴

There are three kinds of sesame seeds: white, black, and light brown. Before sprinkling over salads, deep-fried dishes, or grilled dished, sesame seeds should be toasted in a dry frying pan over medium-low heat. Shake the pan occasionally until the seeds become fragrant and slightly brown. These tiny, flat seeds are also great for baking almond cookies. They are quite reasonably priced when you buy them in Asian supermarkets. Sesame seeds are packaged in plastic bags or in plastic bottles. Once the package has been opened, it should be stored in the freezer and will keep for many months.

Shrimp, dried 蝦米

These tiny shelled, salted shrimp have a pungent taste. They are highly valued by Chinese cooks. Some Chinese people even like to nibble them as a snack. Their unusual flavor will enhance many dishes. Dried shrimp must be soaked in hot water 30 minutes before being added to meat and stir-fried dishes. They are sold by weight in Asian supermarkets and will keep indefinitely if stored in an airtight plastic bag in the freezer.

Sichuan peppercorns 花椒

Don't confuse these with regular peppercorns. Sichuan peppercorns are not peppery hot but give a numbing sensation to the tongue. Sichuan peppercorns are used in red-cooked and stir-fried dishes. Store Sichuan peppercorns as you would other spices.

Sichuan peppercorn powder, toasted 花椒粉

To prepare this powder, put Sichuan peppercorns in a wok or frying pan over medium heat and stir-fry without oil for 5 to 6 minutes, stirring constantly. Let cool and grind the peppercorns in a blender or coffee grinder. Put the ground peppercorns in a sifter to obtain the finer powder. Store the powder in the refrigerator, where it will keep for months.

Sichuan preserved mustard green stems 四川榨菜
This specialty of Sichuan Province is made from a particular mustard green that has many knobby stems. The knobby stems are preserved in salt and chili powder. They can be washed if they are too salty or too hot. They come in whole pieces, chunks, and slices; pre-shredded in cans, jars, and vacuum packages; and loose in large tubs. Store unused Sichuan preserved mustard green stems in the refrigerator for months.

Snow peas 雪豆
Snow peas are also called pea pods. Flat, crisp and green, they are used mainly in stir-fried dishes and soups. Snap off the stem ends and remove the strings on both sides, then parboil very briefly. Frozen snow peas are available, but the quality is much worse. Fresh snow peas will keep in the refrigerator for two weeks.

Sour mustard greens 酸菜
Sour mustard greens are similar to pickles in America. Whole mustard greens, with the leaves and stems, must be parboiled, then drained and put into brine. Cover the container and let the greens ferment until they become sour. Sour mustard greens are sold in cans or by weight in plastic bags and can be purchased at most Asian supermarkets.

Soy sauce 醬油
Soy sauce is one of the most important ingredients in Chinese cooking. There are many brands of soy sauce originating from different regions in China. Soy sauce can vary in flavor and quality from one manufacturer to the next. I recommend Kikkoman soy sauce, a Japanese soy sauce that can be found in most American supermarkets. Once the bottle has been opened, keep it refrigerated.

Soy sauce, dark 老抽
Dark soy sauce is darker, thicker, and sweeter than regular soy sauce. It is ideal for cooking red-cooked meats and stewed dishes, giving them a deep brown, rich color. Shake well before using. Store an opened bottle of dark soy sauce in a cool, dry place.

Soy sauce, thin 生抽
Contrary to what you might think, thin soy sauce is not low in sodium but rather saltier in flavor. It is lighter in color and used to avoid darkening the natural beauty of light-colored food. Once the bottle has been opened, store in a cool, dry place.

Soybean milk 豆漿
Soybean milk is a breakfast staple for Chinese people. It is usually served hot with Chinese flat bread 燒餅 and you tiao 油條 (deep-fried twisted dough sticks). Soybean milk is made from dried soybeans that are soaked and ground in water, then strained. You can buy soybean milk in just about any supermarket in the United States as well as in Asian supermarkets. Homemade soybean milk must be boiled before drinking. Store soybean milk as you would regular milk.

Soybeans, dried 黃豆
These dehydrated, yellow soybeans, about the size of dried peas, are made from fresh soybeans. They are sold in one-pound bags in Asian supermarkets and loosely in health food stores. Stored in a cool, dry place, they will keep for many months.

Soybeans, fresh 毛豆

Fresh soybeans, which come in fuzzy pods, are hard to find in the United States, but frozen ones (with and without pods) are quite delicious. Many people enjoy eating them after they are cooked. Soybeans can also be added to your fried rice.

Star anise 八角

This hard, star-shaped spice has eight points and a licorice flavor. It is used in red-cooked dishes. Star anise is used only as a flavoring agent and should be removed before serving. Store star anise as you would other spices.

Starch, tapioca 西米粉

Tapioca starch comes from the root of the cassava plant. The root is ground into flour and made into granular forms that range from the size of a mustard seed to that of a big pearl. Tapioca starch, also called tapioca flour or powder, is used for thickening sauces and for making shrimp dumpling wrappers when combined with wheat starch. Store it as you would regular flour.

Starch, wheat 澄粉

When the gluten is removed from wheat flour, it becomes wheat starch, which is the main ingredient for making several dim sum dishes. Store it as you would regular flour.

Tiger lily buds (golden needles) 金針

These 2- to 3-inch-long pale-gold brown strands have a slightly sweet flavor. Tiger lily buds come from a special type of lily. They are dry and used as a vegetable. Soak them in boiling water for 10 to 15 minutes, then cut into 1½-inch-long pieces. Store tiger lily buds in a tightly sealed container in a cool place. They will keep for months.

Water chestnuts 馬蹄

These walnut-sized bulbs, which feature a russet-color skin and crisp, white meat, are grown in water fields similar to the way rice is grown. Water chestnuts are not part of the chestnut family. In China they are eaten raw, and in the United States they are often served with cooked dishes. You can buy fresh ones in Asian supermarkets and canned ones in any grocery store. To prepare fresh water chestnuts, wash them, peel off the skin, then slice or dice them. Fresh water chestnuts are crunchy and taste much better than canned ones. Once the can is opened, water chestnuts should be kept in fresh water in a covered container and refrigerated. They will last a week to ten days if the water is changed every other day. Water chestnuts should not be frozen.

Water chestnut powder 馬蹄粉

Water chestnut powder is made from ground water chestnuts. This flour is used for making light pastry or sauces. It is sold in small cellophane bags and can be kept for months in a dry, cool place.

Wine rice 酒釀

Wine rice is made from fermented glutinous rice. Ready-made wine rice is sold in glass jars in Chinese grocery stores. Wine rice must be stored in the refrigerator and keeps for a long time.

Winter melon 冬瓜

This round, green-skinned melon belongs to the squash family and varies in size from 5 to 20 pounds. Smaller amounts can be purchased cut up. Winter melon is a vegetable that is never eaten raw. Remove the seeds and the tough rind. The pulp is translucent and white. Slice thinly and steam or simmer in soup. Keep in refrigerator for several days with cut surfaces covered with plastic wrap.

Wrappers, egg roll 美式春卷皮

Egg roll wrappers are made from flour, eggs, and water. The dough is rolled into thin, pliable sheets by machine. Most Chinese restaurants use egg roll wrappers to make your favorite fried egg rolls. Store the wrappers in an airtight plastic bag in the refrigerator for up to a week or freeze them for up to several months. When working with the wrappers, take out only a few at a time and cover the rest with a damp cloth to prevent them from drying.

Wrappers, spring roll 春卷皮

Spring roll wrappers are made from flour and water. They are either square or round, about 7 inches in diameter. My students prefer to use spring roll wrappers rather than egg roll wrappers when we make spring rolls in class. When deep-fried, spring roll wrappers become crisp and smooth, with a light texture. Store the wrappers in an airtight plastic bag in the refrigerator for up to a week or freeze them for up to several months. When working with the wrappers, take out only a few at a time and cover the rest with a damp cloth to prevent them from drying.

Wrappers, wonton 餛飩皮

Wonton wrappers, like egg roll wrappers, are made from flour, eggs, and water. The thickness of wonton wrappers depends on the manufacturer. I like to use thin wrappers for deep-frying and thick ones for making soup. When working with the wrappers, take out only a few at a time and cover the rest with a damp cloth to prevent them from drying.

COMMENTS FROM MY STUDENTS

I have taken two classes from Professor Jewell, Introduction to Chinese Cooking and Tofu Workshop, both through the adult education program of Arlington County. She provided recipes for all the dishes the students prepared in class. Each was a success because the recipe instructions were clear and the measurements of the ingredients accurate, having been time-tested by Professor Jewell at home and in the many classes she has taught. It is a tribute to Professor Jewell's teaching methods that amateurs such as myself, with little or no previous exposure to Chinese cooking, could unfailingly bring off four or five dishes in an evening that approached restaurant quality in taste and eye appeal.
—Edward Webman, Arlington, VA

Can it possibly be 30 years since I took Rebekah Jewell's Chinese Cooking classes? I guess that when you use something so often, it just becomes a natural part of your life. During the past three decades I have entertained family, friends, business colleagues, and visitors from abroad with Rebekah's recipes. I have shared them countless times with guests who marveled at the meals I could prepare because of her instruction. We all anxiously await Rebekah's book, which will be a welcome relief from thumbing through tattered, old, carefully preserved cooking directions! I also look forward to being able to say to my guests: "Here's a cookbook that shows you exactly how I created this wonderful dinner."
—Liz Coughlin, Haymarket, VA

Rebekah's life in two cultures provides the basis for her unique approach to classic Chinese cuisine: dishes created with elegant style but with a minimum of effort. The delicious recipes that I have used range from the traditional Chicken Lo Mein to the wonderful inventive Paper-Wrapped Shrimp, a particular hit with my husband. She provided a great introduction to Chinese staples, where to find them, and how to choose and prepare them. The advice on selecting cookware and specialty tools, including proper techniques for slicing and chopping, was invaluable. Rebekah's effervescent personality makes her classes great fun. Just how much she loves cooking and sharing it with others is evident and certainly something special.
—Penny Young, Alexandria, VA

My Chinese cooking classes with Rebekah Jewell, which I attended in the mid-70s, proved to be invaluable when I was doing official entertaining at various embassy posts in Africa and the Middle East. The greatest hits were the wonderful cold spicy noodle dish and the soy sauce chicken dish which could be prepared ahead and made large enough to serve dozens of guests. I rejected pleas to give out her recipes for fear of losing my delicious and unique party standbys.
—Beth Kouttab, Chantilly, VA

Rebekah's class was the perfect combination of instruction appropriate for every level of experience, support for a beginner like me, hands-on learning, and fun. She's a master teacher and team-builder, who inspired everyone in class to try something new. She showed us that the many steps of preparation often have short cuts and are always worth it when your friends see – and taste – the final product.
—Judy Judd-Price, Arlington, VA

The cooking class was much more than a cooking class. It was a gathering of friends who learned about Chinese culture and history, food preparation, utensil use, all kinds of wonderful tips for cooking and using ingredients, and who shared a wonderful beyond-expectations afternoon. Rebekah's sparkling personality made the day. Everyone had a truly beautiful afternoon.
—Grace Sines, Laurel, MD

Rebekah is a cooking expert of both simple and elegant Chinese cuisine. Her classes are easygoing guides to food preparation, along with her warmth, humor, and complete knowledge of Chinese cooking. Novice cooks such as myself with no prior experience in Chinese cooking can prepare all of her diverse and delectable dishes presented in a simple step-by-step fashion with easy-to-follow instructions. The original, informative recipes were created by Rebekah from her extensive knowledge and experience of Chinese cooking. With their simple directions, they can produce dishes that look and taste like they were prepared by an experienced cook.
—Gloria A. Toner, Fairfax, VA

I have always had an interest in cooking and wanted to take some ethnic cooking classes, so I signed up with Fairfax County for a Chinese cooking class. Rebekah taught this class, and I collected an incredible amount of information in just one class. The next session I took another class with Rebekah, then another. It's not just a demonstration but a real hands-on class when Rebekah teaches. She provides written recipes and step-by-step instructions along with class involvement. And there are no secrets she won't reveal to the art of successful and delicious Chinese cuisine. Rebekah is a wonderful chef, always striving to make the class fun and informative and everyone as knowledgeable as possible about Chinese cooking before they go out the door. No wonder she is such a success in the county!
—Sandy Bonomi, Alexandria, VA

I was raised on a farm near Staunton, Virginia. I cooked with my mom from the time I was six years old. We never had casserole dishes and stuck pretty much to meat and potatoes or rice and vegetables. As an adult I had tried making stir-fry with mixed results. I took Rebekah's "Cooking Lite" class and discovered that with her recipes I could count on my food tasting delicious each and every time I cooked. I was thrilled with my new recipes. The next class I took from her she even asked what we would like to learn to cook. She showed such respect for each student's needs and desires. I loved taking classes from such an energetic and fun-loving woman.
—Ginsy Shumate, Fairfax, VA

Index